# Tragic Beauty:

# The Lost 1914 Memoirs of Evelyn Nesbit

Evelyn Nesbit
&
Jack Clifford

# Tragic Beauty:

# The Lost 1914 Memoirs of Evelyn Nesbit

### Edited By
### Deborah Dorian Paul

Originally entitled"The Story of My Life"
By Evelyn Thaw

Published by John Long Ltd. London, 1914

Cover photo courtesy of Crystal Lombardo

# Preface to Tragic Beauty:
## The Lost 1914 Memoirs of Evelyn Nesbit

In researching the life of Evelyn Nesbit, I found she had written two memoirs:  One entitled *The Story of My Life*, published in 1914 and the other entitled *Prodigal Days*, published exactly 20 years later in 1934.

Finding a copy of *Prodigal Days* seemed nearly impossible and finding a copy of *The Story of My Life* **WAS** nearly impossible.

It seemed all that remained of Evelyn's *The Story of My Life* (the original title of *Tragic Beauty*) was relegated to ancient microfiche files and some portions of the original book were missing.

Evelyn Nesbit wrote *The Story of My Life* while appearing at London's *Hippodrome* theatre and still married to Harry K. Thaw who, at the time, was unwillingly incarcerated in an insane asylum for the murder of New York's most creative architect—Stanford White.

After piecing together all available portions, I finally arrived at a finished manuscript:  this book is a close approximation to the same manuscript that Evelyn sent to her publishers, John Long Ltd. of London, on a late summer day long ago in 1914.

Comparing the contents of the two memoirs is infinitely interesting.  The 1914 memoirs reveal interesting tidbits of information not mentioned in the 1934 memoirs and *vise versa*.

If you are interested in reading Evelyn Nesbit's 1934 memoirs *Prodigal Days*, ISBN  1-4116-3709-7, it can be purchased online at the following sites: lulu.com/edwardiavictoria, Amazon.Com, Barnes and Noble, or ordered through your local bookstore.

Deborah Dorian Paul

# INTRODUCTION

If there were women or men in the world who do not believe that their lives would make an entrancing story they are either very humble or very clever.

"Commonplace" is a word that is expunged from the lexicon of those who write about themselves. In our arrogance—let me include myself—we imagine that our lives are so far removed from the run of lives, in respect to interest and character, as to be apart.

And we are right, even the most humdrum of us. Who can read Flaubert's *Simple Soul* without realizing this fact? There is no life that is not a fascinating study—always providing that its limner can "carry it across the footlights." The less humdrum the life has been the less skill does the autobiographer require, and it is because my own life has been out of the ordinary that I dare say the task of putting in plain words a rough and, I fear, an amateur chronicle.

I have many friends in the newspaper world both in America and England: unemotional men, whose friendship I value, not so much because they have been able at times to turn the sharp edge of criticism from my unhappy self, but because in many of them I have found a saner judgment, a larger humanity, and broader views than in any other class of men I met. And this has been an astounding thing to me. For your newspaperman, on the surface, is a man of ice; a man pitiless in his analysis and remorseless in his search for facts. Stories that would appall and shock the average person leave him unmoved. He will go right away from a millionaire's luxurious dinner party to the morgue; do a horse show and an electrocution in one day; interview princes and criminals in rotation; and give no indication that he is impressed by either experience.

Yet, for all his seeming callousness, when loosed upon a "story," the newspaperman is very human in his sympathies, and I pay a grateful tribute to some of the journalists of America for the help and encouragement they gave me in the darkest hour of my need.

It flows that amongst my friends of the Press I found many who are willing and anxious to assist me in preparing such a story as this, but although with such assistance the value of the book, as a literary production, might well be materially enhanced, I prefer to wait for a time when I might be able to write, for my own pleasure, the story as I wish to tell it.

I am satisfied that there will be critics who will demur at the necessity for writing the book at all; they will say, "Why rake up the past—a past which cannot be interesting to anybody save the actors, who are fairly unimportant people?" My own view, strengthened by a continuous study of other lives, is that there are no unimportant people in the world. The right to write is almost as incontestable as the right to live, and there will be something in the exaggerated tragedy of the existence that was mine—a lesson for somebody or other.

I hate the cant of the writer who professes to write only for the uplifting of the race, who prepares moral nastiness that the vague "they" shall be benefited, and I dissociate myself from the suggestion that this is a book with an object—yet, as I say, there will be a lesson in this as in every autobiography. It would be a colorless life, indeed, which did not contain this lesson.

Here, then, is the life of Evelyn Thaw.

# Table of Contents

# Chapter I
# MY BEGINNINGS

However anxious one may be to record one's childhood, that period of life is the most elusive.

I lived in Tarentum, on the Allegheny River just outside Pittsburgh. My father was a lawyer. "Win" Nesbit was respected from one end of the country to the other, and had a reputation that extended beyond the line of local celebrity. A charming, genial man; I have only the most tender memories of him, for he died when I was ten, and that is an age when a child begins to form the most roseate impressions of those she has marked down for hero worship.

My childhood was the happiest time of my life. That is the impression I have now. I know that I was a tomboy, very keen on prize-fights (of all things in the world!), and I delighted in promoting combats in secluded spots between children who were very beautiful to me, but who, in the eyes, of my outraged parents, were the most impossible playmates.

My mother is one of the sweetest women I have ever met. Artistic to her fingertips, her home has been a harmonious and attractive place.

I have said she was a beautiful character. She was one of those women whose house is ordered artistically and charmingly. I do not know whether she understood my nature or me. I doubt very much whether any mother is ever entirely in sympathy with her daughter's aspirations. It has been my experience that the son has invariably been the mother's first care, just as the daughter is invariably the father's.

I have a brother with whose characteristics I do not doubt my mother is much better acquainted than with mine. I do not suggest for one moment that there was any violent lack of sympathy between her and myself, nor do I say that had she understood me better, life would have run on different lines. And, if I express the opinion that my brother was the first consideration, I do not do so in an irritated or an aggrieved frame of mind. I believe in the natural order of things, and I am quite content to accept such order without complaint, realizing that had my father lived; my brother would probably have enjoyed the same experience.

I have the fullest admiration for my mother's character. She is altogether a wonderful woman. She is one of those sweet characters who could not plant a dry stick in the earth but that it blossomed; who could make the prettiest things; was eminently efficient in all her household duties; the most perfect and dainty of housewives; the most trusting and believing of creatures.

But she did not understand me. Today, I am probably the greatest enigma that the world offers her. I am outside and beyond the range of her understanding. She is one of those women, who are always willing to believe the best, and quite ready to fear the worst.

I cannot take a convenient and lazy course and put all the blame of the friction upon my ancestry. My mother and I were temperamentally different. I made matters impossible because I was young, headstrong, and willful, filled with the sublime assurance of youth, and opposed by one whose nature was so sweet and so simple that I could without any effort, circumvent her most convincing argument.

I was, as I have said, born in Tarentum, in Pennsylvania, on the Allegheny River. There is a Taranto in Italy, a corruption of the ancient Tarentum, but the town namers of the United States were never purists. When I was eight years old we moved across the river to Allegheny, and lived there for two years.

It was while we were there that my father died. I have only the dimmest recollection of the period that followed. I realized then, with a vague sense of childish discomfort, that it was a period of trouble for my mother.

I do not know exactly in what position my father left her, but my recollection is that my mother had to pay frequent visits to the court regarding my father's affairs.

At first, we seemed to be in some prosperity, but afterwards there was a great deal of worry. Whatever money my mother had was gone, and it was necessary for us to rent a few rooms in the house to outsiders.

That seemed a fairly easy method of keeping the wolf from the door, but somehow, it never worked smoothly. Mother was always worried about the rent she had to pay, and still more worried about the rent she did not always get. And there were times when we felt the pinch very acutely and did not get enough to eat.

The next move, I remember, was to my grandmother's. We went and lived with her. I think at that time we had no money whatever, and my earliest recollections of Pittsburgh are almost as painful as my later recollections.

Poverty is very impatient and fretful. People who are poor find their salvation in action, and, since a woman's sphere is a limited one, and scope for initiative necessarily small, mother again rented a house on 5th South Highland Avenue, Pittsburgh, and let most of the rooms to other people.

I remember that my mother, my little brother, and myself had to sleep in one room. There was no place for any of us elsewhere. Yet, despite all these discomforts, and all the sacrifices we made, the new house and the new arrangement did not pay any better than had our house in Allegheny.

In theory it showed excellent profits, but in practice there was the difficulty of collecting the rents, and I just remember that after a little while we had more trouble, and that the furniture had to be sold.

It was then that a very good friend of mother's came to our rescue, and paid the man to whom we owed rent. Mother had made up her mind that she would leave Pittsburgh and go to

Philadelphia. She was very artistic, and she hoped to get a position as a designer. We were sent to an aunt, and afterwards to a family that my mother had known in Pittsburgh.

It is curious how memory shapes the events that are of such paramount importance and that are destined to play so great a part in one's career.

I remember that rail journey that my brother and I took alone; how we were put in the charge of the conductor, and the trouble we had with the family cat, which I insisted upon taking with me to our new home. Every conductor that came aboard wanted to put the poor cat off. It was a weepy journey for me. Finally we got to Philadelphia, where my mother and another lady met us at the depot.

I was between thirteen and fourteen at the time; just old enough to take an intelligent interest in my parent's affairs. I do not remember exactly what idea I had as to our future when I went to Philadelphia. I probably thought my mother had already secured an appointment; but I found that she was living in one room in a small boardinghouse and that the position of designer, the securing of which was to retrieve the family fortunes, had not yet materialized.

Clever as she was in the making and planning of clothes, the people who employed designers wanted one who had practical experience on the commercial side of the business. They wanted somebody who had been to Paris, who had studied and had at their fingertips the latest mode, and poor mother, with all the best intentions in the world, could not lay claim to so large and varied an experience.

What little money we had began to go again. My brother was sent back to a convenient aunt living outside Pittsburgh, and we moved to a place in Arch Street.

From my point of view, this was the most momentous of our moves. The boardinghouse in Arch Street marked the beginning of my independent career. Until now I had been a follower—a being whose life was directed by whims or the circumstances of another.

Hitherto, I and the rest of the world had revolved around my mother. In my eyes, my mother held the central attraction around which animated creation gyrated. Arch Street represented the period of transition, a stage during which the center of attraction slowly but surely shifted.

It was there I met a Mrs. Darach, who was an artist. She was attracted by my face, and asked me if I would sit as a model for her. The idea attracted me. It seemed to me at that time to be a wonderful thing that anybody should want to paint a picture of me. It was really a wonderful joke, and I was as proud as though I, myself, combined all the genius of Michelangelo and Rosa Bonheur.[1]

I learned in that time the supreme value of patience. Enthusiasm for being painted died with an aching neck, and I found myself with a yearning desire to get away from the position in which the artist put me, to move my head exactly in the direction she did not wish me to look, and to fidget at moments when it was essential that I should keep quite still.

Here, then, began the great education—an education that served me in such good stead in later years. Other artists would drop into the studio in Chestnut Street, and one woman who came was very anxious that I should sit for her. Mrs. Darach, however, pointed out that I was not a professional model; but the other lady artist was very insistent.

"Why," she said, "I know lots of girls who are earning quite good money by posing for illustrators of magazines."

I had never thought of the possibility of making an income in this way. It seemed to me absurd that people should take money for being painted. I spoke to mother about it, but she did not offer any objection, and thus it came about that from

---

[1]Rosa Bonheur (1822-1899) a French artist, who was the most successful female painter of her time. Bonheur became known for her paintings of domesticated animals and scenes of rural life.

Mrs. Darach I went to other artists, and slowly but surely began to form quite a connection among the artists who were in the building.

I posed mostly for heads, particularly for children's heads, and at first for the lady artists. There were four in that building who used me as a model for illustrated stories in the best-known magazines.

I grew in patience, and the work came easy. Beyond the fact that most of the people who drew me were, as I say, women, there were one or two men artists whose names I do not remember.

When I was in full swing, we decided to move to New York, and my artist friends gave me letters of introduction, one of which was to Mr. Carroll Beckwith. Mother went to New York, and she sent me back to Pittsburgh. Even then our circumstances were so strained that it was necessary for my father's friend to obtain a rail pass for me.

I had to go back to get Howard, my little brother. I was there for a few weeks, and we went on, by way of Allegheny, to New York.

My mother would never cease in her efforts to secure a position as designer, but in New York she had no greater success than she had in Philadelphia. The main objections that barred her in the smaller city were against her in New York.

We had secured a room on Twenty-second Street—a little backroom on the second floor. Here we lived, and again felt the pinch of poverty. There were days when my sole meal consisted of a biscuit and a cup of coffee.

Try as she would, my mother did not succeed in securing even a minor position with a firm of dress designers. Everywhere the same answer was returned, the same questions asked: "Had she been to Paris recently? Had she similar experiences with other firms?"

It was in desperation that mother remembered the letter of introduction to Mr. Carroll Beckwith. In Philadelphia, during the month of December 1900, my artist friends sent me to a photographer to secure a number of studies of my head. Armed with these photographs, mother called upon Mr. Beckwith.

The artist was pleased with the photographs. He told her that she could bring me up to the studio, because he felt pretty sure that he would be able to give me work. A personal inspection satisfied him, and he offered me posing for two mornings every week.

"You are not the sort of girl," he said kindly, "that should go knocking at studio doors. I will give you some letters of introduction to a representative artist in New York."

This he did. I remember one was Mr. F. S. Church, and Mr. Church gave me letters to Herbert Morgan, and Mr. and Mrs. Hyneman, and Carl Blenner and I posed for all of them.

The work was fairly light. The poses were not particularly difficult. They mainly wanted me for my head. I never posed for the figure, in the sense that I posed in the nude. Sometimes I would be painted as a little Eastern girl in a costume of a Turkish woman, all vivid coloring, with ropes and bangles of jade about my neck and arms.

In a sense, it was my work as an artist's model that first brought me into the public eye. I didn't know that to be brought into the public eye is the happiest of experiences. Wilde has said that a woman, like a country, is happiest when she has no history.

I remember in New York a reporter came down to the house to see me. It was a novel experience, and one that considerably flattered me; it was the first of many interviews that were to be my lot. Mother showed him a photograph that had been taken in Philadelphia. It is a curious fact that I have do not possess a single one of these pictures, though it is not such a long time since they were taken. A posed photograph of me was printed

9

in an evening paper in New York, with a complimentary caption underneath, and from that time onward I saw many reporters, all of whom were anxious to get a photograph for their papers.

The Sunday*American* published several of them, two big pages, and it was only natural that printed photographs should be followed by a succession of offers to go on the stage.

I suppose such an experience, falling to a young girl unused to publicity and with little knowledge of the world, would be sufficient to turn her head. But I was immensely sane in those days. I attribute this to the fact that I had read more that most girls my age. My father had an excellent library, and I had been a most omnivorous reader. I laugh to myself when I think of the literary puzzle I tackled. I am more than astounded to realize that I not only read, but also enjoyed, many books that a child might reasonably be supposed to think more than a little difficult. But the efforts I made in those early days to master such classics as came my way provided a sort of mental gymnastic that enabled me to secure a sense of proportion, the one sense which spells salvation to a girl upon whom is lavished the subtle flattery of publicity. This, and my own taste for a healthy, open-air life, enabled me to take a normal view of things. I have always loved the fields and woods and every beast that walks or creeps or crawls. There are no phenomena of nature that are not beautiful to me.

A healthy girl does most of her dreaming by night, and if I did any dreaming at all in the daytime it was not of the career that lay ahead of me. A girl's dreams are never practical, and the freakish being that looks forward to a life of mending and minding — the ultimate fate of the vast majority of dreamers — is a type of girl yet to be discovered.

I was not insensible to the possibilities of a career on the stage, but all my enthusiasm was for the present — the immediate joy of penetrating that mysterious world that lay beyond the proscenium arch.[2]

Already I had found a little world outside my own; already I found myself looking back upon the life domestic with the interests and curiosity that a mountaineer reserves for the plains he has quitted.

---

[2] A **proscenium arch** is a square frame around a raised stage area in traditional theatres. It creates a "window" within which the play is performed.

# Chapter II
# THE CALL OF THE STAGE

I had met men and women with aspects peculiarly their own, with an outlook upon life that so differed from the outlook of commonplace folk I had mingled with, as to almost suggest that they were another species of biped. I felt I was learning things, and I have always had a passion for acquiring knowledge. If I had been a man I should have been an explorer. To me

> "Something calls beyond the ranges
> . . . Come and find me. . ."

My interest in life, never flagging, grew in intensity. I was permeated with the delight of living. Every day held a mystery, revealed a beautiful experience.

So when I am asked in what spirit I approached the stage and the career it offered me, I say I approached the stage as I would a virgin forest today, with a bubbling sense of happiness in the revelations that it would open to me. I was not stage-struck in the accepted sense. I never thought of the audience and what charm I might exert over them — I did not anticipate huge triumphs in floral tributes handed across the footlights, nor did I dream dreams of laudatory newspaper notices. I was supremely indifferent as to the position I might occupy in the profession; it was enough to me that I should be one with the people of the new world, privy to their lives, their habits of thought and speech. I should be "in it."

Offers came to me from all manner of people promising me all manner of success, dazzling prospects of distant fame were held before my eyes, with the newspapers exclaiming I should command high salaries, I should star, I should be the most talked-of-woman in America — all these promises, light-heartedly given, came to me, and I remember that I was not impressed. I was only interested in the actual getting there. One letter from a manager asking for my services at twenty dollars a week would have eclipsed all other communications had I not been practical enough to realize that a freakish notoriety was not desirable from any point of view.

The greatest advancement, apart from an inborn desire for enlargement of life, lay in the very material fact that the stage life would enable me to make a double income. I could pose by day and appear on the stage by night. The dollars counted horribly, for I had tasted privation and was anxious to put myself as far distant from a repetition of that dismal circumstance as I could.

I do not think that my mother was overly anxious for me to adopt the stage as my profession, but fate was moving me inexorably in the direction I was to take.

Every day the new life became a more tangible possibility, and when, at length, I entered the unpromising stage door it seemed less of a new experience than an introduction to a life with which I was already familiar.

I had a letter from Mr. Marks, who was a theatrical manager. He was very anxious that I should go on the stage and promised me that he would do all he could to make me famous. These letters used to come addressed to us, but we paid little attention to them, but afterwards he wrote saying that he could get me a position in the *Florodora*, and some time later, through a girl I knew, I met him and secured a letter of introduction to John C. Fishell, who was at that time manager of the *Florodora* company.

From this point, the stage became a practical issue. I overruled mother's objections and went with her one day to Mr. Fishell's office. He took a long look at me. He was a pleasant, genial man, blessed with a sense of humor, and he burst into a fit of laughter.

"So you want to be an actress," he said, with mock solemnity. "I am running a theatre, not a baby farm. Why," he went on, "if I took you in the *Florodora* I should have the Gerry Society[3] on my track. No, my child, I cannot rob the cradle."

What was amusing to Mr. Fishell did not amuse me, and I was so upset at seeing all my dreams shattered that I wept and would have gone away at once. He looked at me for a moment.

"There is a rehearsal going on upstairs," he said, "and if you would care to come to it and look at it — "

That was sufficient to arrest my tears. Would I go up and look at it — would I enter that new world of mine? I could have asked for no greater, wonderful experience. The stage manager took me upstairs, and I got my first glimpse of the life and the work.

I think I was so enthusiastic that even the fear of the Gerry Society faded from his mind. When I got back to the office Mr. Fishell asked me if I could dance. I said "yes" a little fearfully. I had learned dancing at a school in Pittsburgh. He sent for a woman who came to the piano and played. The stage manager was keen on my coming into the theatre, but Mr. Fishell was not so enthusiastic, and said he should let me know.

"The fact is," he said, frankly, "the only chance of you're coming on the stage is for you to be a little reticent as to what your age is. If you like to do this I am willing to give you a trial; you can come tomorrow and rehearse."

I went home in the seventh heaven of delight; for one long month the rehearsals went on.

So many people have told me that their first glimpse of the stage from the business side of the footlights was disappointing that I hesitate to give my impressions lest I be regarded as other than normal. I do not blame the newcomer whose heart sinks at the shabbiness of the apparatus of acting.

---

[3]In 1875 Eldridge Thomas Gerry founded, with the help of Henry Bergh, the New York Society for the Prevention of Cruelty to Children (sometimes called the Gerry Society).

A set that represents a beautiful garden from the front of the house, is a drab, tattered, and discolored stage prop. Lovely dresses as seen from the auditorium are too often bedraggled and soiled on close inspection. The stage itself is a bare, cold barn of a floor, inexpressibly dull when seen in the unromantic light of early morning.

All these things I understand without seeing.

Even today I see the stage and its machinery with the spectator's eye rather than with eye of the participant. As I saw it, it was a beautiful place, a very wonder-house of joy. I remember the eagerness with which I began my work, my anxiety to perfect myself for the unimportant duties that were mine.

There could not be sufficient rehearsals to suit me. I wanted to rehearse all the time. Everybody seemed so kind to me— and indeed was. Girls I did not know did everything they could to help me along, and though I do not think unkindness on the part of my fellow players would have altered my determination to work on the stage, yet it is certain that their treatment of me gave me so roseate a view of my new profession, that the tawdriness of the material side of stage life was entirely obliterated from my vision.

And here let me deal with an aspect of stage life that forever excites the moralist. Has it a corrupting influence on the young? I speak for myself when I say it did not corrupt me. If being brought into contact with people who are loose of speech, or who have exaggerated views on the flexibility of morals is corruption, then the streets of New York, of Paris, of London, of any great city, are unfit for the young girl.

There is camaraderie on the stage that entails a certain freedom of speech and frankness in dealing with the relationships that exist between people, but there is also the protection that comes from the destruction of illusion.

And there is, too, a very keen appreciation of duty towards the innocent. There is a code that protects the child and stands between her and knowledge of evil, and in no other branch of life have I seen such anxiety displayed to hide ugly truths from the novitiate.

Here is an example of how a girl can live in the very midst of things without fully understanding their significance.

I remember that in those early days I used to envy a sextette of beautiful girls who had a chorus number of their own. I used to stand in the wings, watching them dancing gracefully the slow movements of the scene and wonder a little ruefully whether I should ever be tall enough or skillful enough to do the work they were doing. For, in my innocence, I regarded them as the most wonderful part of the show, and certainly the best paid. "For." I argued, "How could they wear such lovely clothes off the stage, and such beautiful pearls on, unless they received a salary in proportion to their charms?"

I must have mentioned my view to several people, but not one of them attempted to lift the veil that hid realities from my eyes. The stage was indeed a wonderful world, its people a people apart. One looked at life from a new angle and saw men and women as from another lane. I was impressed by the frank egotism of the girls—a quality that is neither to be despised nor condemned, for they merely put into words what their sisters of the other world think. They have mastered the trick of thinking aloud, and found speech an excellent and soothing substitute for thought, which is one reason why actresses apparently seem so inconsistent.

I found it took years of study before I could disentangle the real intentions of a girl from her expressed, and often vehemently expressed, view. I have heard people—and men especially—who have complained bitterly of the inconsistency and deceptive powers of girls engaged on the stage.

Laws that have no exact counterpart in other branches of life govern the girls on the stage. The way of the ballet girl, or of the chorus girl, since ballets are now so unfashionable—does not change. Her code, her method is unchanged through all

17

the centuries. The girls of Thais[4] are the girls of the modern show. They have the same thoughts, the same ambitions, and the same peculiar charm. I am getting outside of myself now and examining my friends of other days without any relation to myself.

You must remember that the average girl who joins a chorus is one with little or no opportunity for tasting the comforts of existence. Their early days are spent very often amid the most distressing circumstances. There is nothing discreditable in this fact, but it is unfortunate that girls who have not the benefit of an education often disregard the fact that there is no discreditable aspect to poverty. They disguise their true selves for fear people will look down upon them for having been brought up in disadvantaged circumstances.

Half the artificiality of the theatre is due to a monstrous misconception as to what is essential in a woman. A girl with no great stability of mind, very easily has her angles of vision displaced. It is her first object to secure a line of reputable parentage, then on to a few romantic circumstances which lead to their present position is but a step. The formula does not vary considerably. A ruined father — a life of noble self-sacrifice and eventually the theatre. These are the stories that one hears from the girls of the chorus.

It is at first glance amusing; at second glance and from all subsequent points of view, it is very pathetic. A little county mouse that finds herself amid her smartly clad, and even bejeweled sisters, undergoes an ordeal beside which a mere appearance before the footlights is nothing.

The chorus girl does not vary in any country that I have seen. There is a significant lack of ambition to succeed in the profession into which she has intruded herself, and whatever ambition she possesses, is concentrated upon a desire to shine before her newly found friends.

---

[4]Thais was a famous Greek courtesan who lived during the time of Alexander the Great and accompanied him on his campaigns.

To girls who come from the quiet and often painfully disciplined households of America, the freedom, the gaiety, the life and the color are irresistible. These cheery parties, so hilarious and so apparently innocent, appeal with extraordinary force to the young girl who is still in a stage of cubdom that makes life something to be accompanied by noise and great laughter.

"There is something about the stage that seems to put veracity and honor to sleep," said one man. It was the sort of wild statement that a particularly voluble chorus girl might have made, and the truth, as ever, lay somewhere in the middle.

The stage girl is a frank appellant for admiration, particularly the admiration of men. She sings, she dances, and she dresses with this central thought in mind: "I must arouse the interest of men."

Women in other walks of life do exactly the same thing, because they are obeying the same instinct that animates the chorus girl. Their invitation may be more subtle and intimate, but they are not attempting to span the immense gulf that stretches between the stage and their audience.

A chorus girl must impress a general and pleasing sense of her womanliness upon the men she has come to please. There is neither opportunity, nor is there machinery, for conveying her individuality across the footlights. Here I may say that the ideal chorus girl is one who must also be pleasing to women, for women are attracted by a certain phase of femininity that finds expression on the stage.

The opportunity comes to her after the show, and yet it is the new chorus girl that meets her admirer. Too often the meeting is disappointing to a man who secures his ideal picture of the girl when she was one of many. I am always sorry for the girl, and have very little patience with the disillusioned man, who then begins all over again reconstructing his ideal as he discovers the illusive charm that attracted him to this or that particular member of the chorus.

I cannot recall at this moment in exactly what direction my ambitions ran. I think they were very gauche and nebulous. Perhaps the example of desiring that I might become a member of the sextette conveys a fairly faithful picture of my wishes. I am quite satisfied in my mind that they never took definite shape. A woman who lives in the past sacrifices her beauty; a woman who lives in the present sacrifices her conscience.

In those days I lived very much in the present, and if conscience is an uneasy stirring as to one's future then I certainly had no conscience. I do not intend to sacrifice my appearance for the worry of recollecting the wisdom of my attitude at that moment.

Apart from the fascination of actual stage work, the hurry and excitement of preparations for the performance, the exhilaration of the music, the plaudits of the audience, and the hurry and rush of change made at breathless speed all combined to stimulate my interest in life.

There was another life that lay beyond the theatre, and was, so to speak, an appendage of it. There were parties, parties given by boys to girls, just as innocent and just as frolicsome as they would have been had they been given in the later hours of the morning, and had they been prepared for college girls instead of for girls of the chorus. We always went in bunches to these parties. One girl would invite the other, and we would go off to a café for supper, and afterwards to some apartment where we could dance, and if it was the early hours of the morning before we dispersed our several ways, we were just as bright and just as fresh as when we had started at night.

I would emphasize the perfect innocence of these frolics. I would go so far as to say that even when the frolic took the form of literally going home with the milk, as they say in England, there was nothing in them but harmless amusement.

Mother took an old-fashioned view of these early morning arrivals, and the old-fashioned view through all ages has been the view of people who no longer desire to do the things that they criticize. It often seems, when one listens to the admonition of one's elders and betters, that one is gazing — with some awe, I confess — upon the relic of an age which knew not frolic or unconventional action, and one has ever a sense of being a product of a novel and decadent generation. But I rather think my analysis of old-fashioned ness is nearer the mark, and there may come a day when I myself will look with stern disapproval upon a younger generation and its follies. I trust, however, that my outlook will be from a newer and better world.

And yet, thinking these things over, I agree with mother entirely. Her temperament was different from mine, and I cannot in my wildest moments imagine her in her wildest moments greeting the dawn from the wrong end of the day.

Let me forget my mother's nervous fears about the stage and its people. For me this theatreland was a *terra incognita*, and such lands have a charm of their own. The artistic set had been an equally and unknown land. But I have explored it to my satisfaction: it was now familiar ground. I had learned many things — curious things that might never ordinarily occur to a girl who was inspired to vacuity by the monotony of sittings.

I had learned to pursue the errant thought that flies into the mind and out again. I had followed such thoughts through fantastic avenues and had secured angles of vision that perhaps I should not ordinarily have secured.

Have you ever noticed the thought in the eyes of a pictured girl? Have you ever seen a man model whose eyes were not vacant? The artist's model is either an auto-hypnotist or a mental gymnast — I think I was the latter.

I certainly went out to the new life better equipped than I had been before my introduction to the artistic world. I had "worked things out" with some clarity of vision, and I knew exactly what I wanted.

It has been laid at the door of the theatrical profession that its men are artificial and its women without sincerity. An English actor told me that, so far as his country is concerned, the change is due entirely to the fact that those who promulgate it are provincial people, who object to the more cultured accent of the London actor. I see a more intelligent reason in the fact that the people who talk so easily and so readily of artificiality are people to whom everything associated with the stage is anathema.

Stage folk are ordinary people with extraordinary sympathies. They are very like other people, in that they love to talk about their work.

A friend of mine was talking very disparagingly of actors to me in London. After a while, when the subject had taken another turn, he said apologetically: "You can see I come from a theatrical stock — I am talking about myself!"

But, unfortunately, this trait is not peculiar to stage folk. I know of no subject more interesting to the average man than himself. It is generally the one subject on whom he can speak with authority, and one of the few which incites his imagination to greater things. All men lie when speaking of themselves, and, however good or pious they may be, they exaggerate their own qualities.

It matters little anyway just so long as they are talking of themselves. Choose the hour when working people are returning from their labors and sit with them in a car or on the subway. Their conversation shows the universality of the practice of self-appreciation. They are talking of themselves, of their daily achievements. The Mikes, Henrys, and Jimmies of life are telling what they said to the foreman and the ganger[5],

---

[5] British term for a foreman of a gang of workers.

and what the boss said to them—and the story as it is told invariably reflects to the credit of the teller.

Go to lunch at a restaurant mainly used by businessmen. They are talking about themselves, of this smart deal or that, of how they hoodwinked the Hoggenheimers, or of how Old Man Hoggenheimer tried and failed to hoodwink them. Go right to the very top and hear the captains of industry talking. It is of their own work they speak in moments of relaxation. The only people I have ever met who never talk about themselves are Japanese, bank robbers, and ambassadors.

That actors and actresses are superstitious is a fact. Some highly moral person has discovered that superstition is the negation of religion, but that is as absurd as it can be. All people are superstitious. In some it forms a substitute for religious belief, and in others it is an appendage to faith. When people talk of superstition and its relationship to the stage my mind goes to a production with which I was afterward associated.

It was to be a wonderful production, and the most wonderful of all the features was to be a very complicated piece of machinery, which was to be produced in the most important of ensembles. The last rehearsal was called, and the piece was running as smoothly as it could run when there walked on the stage a cat, and it was a black cat!

Now a black, cat, by all accepted theories of superstition, is a lucky animal.[6] She (or he) is the Western equivalent of the Hindu's sacred cow. She is something to be propitiated, to be treated with courtesy amounting to sycophancy. For a black cat makes all the difference between a besieged box-office and an auditorium sprinkled with bored people.

The rehearsal stopped.

---

[6] In Europe and many parts of the world a black cat is considered a good luck token. If one crosses your path, it is an omen of money to come.

All eyes turned to the cat. The eyes of the chorus glistened. The eyes of the principals sparkled — the producer just glared respectfully, but alas! Resentfully, at that black cat.

She, poor soul, unconscious of the tremendous effect of her appearance, raised her tail and yowled dismally.

"Kitty — Kitty — Kitty!" whispered the chorus excitedly.

"Kitty — Kitty — Kitty!" called the principals frantically.

The big producer stood in the center of the stage and said nothing. He just glared at that cat.

For a moment she hesitated, then turned to the wings; and the producer sighed happily.

"Let us get on," he said; and the leading lady sat at a table in the center of the stage to deliver her lines. But the black cat changed her mind. She came back to the stage slowly and with dignity.

The rehearsal went on, one eye of the chorus on the cat and the other on the producer. The leading woman spoke her part a little disjointedly because she was looking at the cat; the producer did not notice what she said because he was looking at the cat too.

She advanced to the center of the stage and jumped up into the leading lady's lap.

There were ecstatic murmurs from a chorus, a delighted coo from the favored lady, an exclamation that was ecstatic but not delighted from the producer, and the cat snuggled down apparently to sleep.

"I guess we'll cut that cat out for a while," said the producer.

Looks of horror and pain met him.

"Why, Mr. —, don't you know that a black cat brings luck?" asked the leading lady reproachfully.

The big man fidgeted.

"Let the call boy hold the luck for a spell," he suggested; but no, the cat must not be disturbed. Eventually the cat, condescended to get down and return to the wings, lured thither by a saucer of milk.

Again the rehearsal proceeded. The piece of complicated machinery that was the crux of the play was brought to the center of the stage, the chorus sang, the chorus danced, the leading lady did both, and the producer in his white sweater yelled his comments through a megaphone—and then the cat came back.

She came back at the most critical moment of the rehearsal, when the producer's rumpled hair told eloquently of his pessimism. That cat came back and leaped lightly on to the top of the automatic fountain (as I think it was), and began to wash its impudent face.

"Get that cat out before I kill it!" roared the producer. They argued with him, they pleaded with him. The leading woman went so far as to say that if the cat went she would make a duet of it and go too. It was bad luck to drive away a black cat— horrible things would happen—people would die—the play would fall—the theatre would burn down.

Once more the saucer of milk was requisitioned, and the cat, albeit reluctantly, was lured to the wings.

Once more the rehearsal proceeded, but the air was charged with electricity. Again the moment of crisis came, the chorus was in the throes of a complicated movement—and the cat returned.

She walked along the stage, a happy, frolicsome, joyous cat. She stopped to play tag with a property garland of roses, and then she hopped on to the fountain and sat enthroned amidst the tinsel and glass of the apparatus. For one moment the producer stood petrified with rage, then he took a quick step forward. Up came his big foot—he missed the cat, but the gorgeous fountain was a ruin of wire and glass and canvas! The piece was a success.

My homecoming was often attended with a certain apprehension that is not unknown to the most sedate of us. I can hear mother's reproachful "OH, Evelyn!" now. I have often heard criticisms of what to her must have been my outrageous conduct sketched in even stronger terms and at greater length, but as I snuggled in between sheets, full of sudden healthy sleepiness, oblivious to criticism and much that might have been helpful to me in my after life, I was concerned only in a very natural desire to recuperate my exhausted vitality.

Party succeeded party, as I have said, girls were taken out by men of all kinds and of all ages, and they very soon discovered in me a child who had particularly childish interests. They were amused by my passion for mechanical toys, and in those days I heard nothing to which I might take exception. Indeed, the conversation was generally so innocuous as to be almost banal, that is the impression I have today.

Happy times are hard to remember, great sorrows are the red stamp in the index book of life. A happy childhood may be expressed in the character of he or she who has been fortunate enough to experience it. It leaves no greater memory than does a comfortable dream, and only now and again by some trick of memory can I recall the men and women who contributed to that careless period of life which was all white roses and down.

Some of the girls drank because they thought it was the thing to do, and was part of their lives. It was good fun to feel the exhilarating sense that strong waters bring. A cocktail was less a pleasure than part of the ritual of good fun; champagne was something rather amusing. I doubt whether any of the girls liked it, but it was seeing life, and since nobody took very much, little harm was done.

The days passed rapidly; new and pleasant people came flocking into my life and disappeared again; some came back and impressed themselves upon my mind, a few, very few, remained as permanent landmarks, but the vast majority are pleasant ghosts.

26

All went cheerily and happily: posing as a model by day, rushing to the play at night, the parties that so often ended when the day had begun anew, all these pleasant things made this an extremely happy period of my life.

Then into my life came Stanford White.

# CHAPTER III
## STANFORD WHITE

How shall I speak of Stanford White?  If I took a conventional view, if I followed the path which popular prejudice would have me tread, I should speak of him with loathing as something unclean, some ugly excrescence of humanity, the very thought of which was horrible.  I am looking at him now across a gulf of years — years charged with sorrow and mental anguish; I am looking at him, from the standpoint of a woman, and a worldly woman.  We judge human beings by their large worth to the world rather than by their individual foibles.

The judgment of the moment is seldom a sane one or a just one.  Wilde might have been obliterated from the world of literature, and his books placed on the *Index Expurgator* if the decision had rested with the people of England in the days of his trial.  Sheridan by some standards was an incorrigible drunkard, Pitt a hopeless gambler unfit to be trusted with the finances of his country, and Alexander Hamilton was a libertine.

I cite these examples at random because they were great men, just as Stanford White was a great man.

That is how I see him after all these years.  That he did me a wrong, that from certain moral standards he was perverse and decadent, does not blind my judgment.

Stanford White was a great man, a man of tremendous powers and capabilities; large and generous in his dealing with his fellows; brilliant as an artist and scholar; kindly to a degree in his relations with those who needed his kindness.  My remembrance of him is a sad but appreciative one.

I met Stanford White at a supper party.  He had a friend in the chorus, who invited me to meet him.  It was no novel thing to meet new people — it was, as I have made clear, a very usual circumstance, and I attached no great importance to the outing, save that I was going to meet a great person of whom I had heard, and who, by all accounts, was a very clever man. And let me say here that cleverness in a man or a woman has always been the supreme attraction.

Never once in my life have I found the slightest pleasure in the commonplace—a leisure that is revered entirely for those favored folk who get a good amount of placid joy in finding things as they expect them, and expect very little.

My first experience of Mr. White was that he was very unprepossessing, very kindly, and that he was safe. He did not treat me with any great ceremony, but he was courteous, attentive, and took an interest in my life. There was something subtly flattering to me in this attention and interest, and I found myself listening to him with a satisfaction that few people have given to me.

He exercised an almost fatherly supervision over what I ate, and was particularly solicitous as to what I drank. He was mildly reproving, gently bantering, a man who kept one smiling with his own good humor or interested in his own experience. Everybody had spoken so well of him, and he was undoubtedly a genius in his art. He had met my mother and knew something of our history, and he was keenly interested in my adventures in the artistic world.

He had a trick of suggesting disparagement without expressing it.

What seems so difficult for people to understand—and particularly women—is that at the trial or the subsequent proceedings, I never expressed a deep-rooted horror of Stanford White. Neither then nor now can I conjure a pose such as the conventional world demands. White is to me a memory as of a great experience. One remembers an earthquake without blaming or condemning the seismic forces that produced the phenomena. White was an earthquake that shattered to the foundations the fabric of innocence.

I can see him now with his big, broad frame, his hair all burnished copper—it stood up like velvet pile—his easy manner, his ready laugh. He was a compendium of information on all subjects, likely and unlikely. He was an authority and a teacher.

Some men keep jealously locked in their bosom the best side of their lives; and I observed this of men in their relations with women, if they boast they boast unworthily. If they speak of their accomplishments they lie. Stanford White suggested his own genius by his appreciation of genius, contemporary—and past. He was one of those men gifted by Nature beyond the average. He had all the enthusiasm of the amateur combined with the sure skill of the perfect workman. Books, pictures, and science in its most fascinating form—he had them at his fingertips. He had tremendous reserves; some men may be skimmed and left empty, but no man ever plumbed the depths of Stanford's knowledge.

If this sounds too enthusiastic an appreciative of the man, let me say that I am speaking the truth about him. Not even for the purpose of pleasing those who demand, according to the rules of melodrama, a bitterer and more prejudiced view, I can only represent him as he was. Of his failing we know—it was his one failing.

> "A grievous fault
> And grievously hath Caesar answered it."

He was a libertine—and quixotic. He was a generously big man—infinitely mean; he was kind and tender—and preyed upon the defenseless. There are, I am satisfied, such paradoxes in human nature as Stanford White offered. He would shiver at a solecism; a crude expression offended him; yet in some things he was shameless. He was a benevolent vampire.

At this moment, after years of calm reflection, and viewing all things in the light of subsequent experience, I would not dare say of him that he ruined my life. Who indeed dare say that any one act in a lifetime of action ruined them?

31

He merely made a way for me, a painful way, not the smoothest nor the least exciting, but a way that was inevitably mine. It is not for me to judge, nor for you. If you will explain by what system a man takes a train to Baltimore and meets his childless and unloved wife at the depot, and another man goes to his happy family in Chicago and is killed in a railway accident, I will explain why I did not rail at the fate which led me to Stanford White, to hours of made regret, and to days of extraordinary interest.

It is profitless to ask "Why?" of fate; weak to accept its decrees without inquiry. The middle way is the way of human nature, which is to squeal at the moment and blame some other victim for the jostling he could not help.

Men like Stanford White loom into life. I have only a cloudy recollection of when his name was first mentioned to me. I have only the dimmest remembrance of our first meeting. He was terribly old to me—I think in those days all men over twenty-five were old.

I was eager for friendship. As I have said, I loved everybody and everything. I though the stage was a lovely place, and everybody a kindly Sir Galahad.

Men like Stanford White—I am speaking now of the baser Stanford White with which the world is better acquainted—reduce their methods to an exact science.

White had a formula that apparently never varied. He found girls easy prey. He had the appearance and the manner that readily impressed and deceived them. I have said that by nature he was a kindly man. It was not necessary for him to play a part when he assumed the paternal attitude toward those he marked down. It was so easy to accept candies from this benevolent man, and in my case an easier matter, since my tastes were very childish, and I grew ecstatic over mechanical toys. My fascination for toys was a great joke among my acquaintances—so great a joke that Mr. White found the shortcut to my affections.

It must not be thought that my introduction to Stanford White was haphazard. Almost every invitation to a party was not automatically accepted. My mother exercised considerable surveillance over my comings and goings. She guided me to a very large extent. At first she would not consent to my going to the party at which I was destined to meet Stanford White. She did not know, any more than I, that Stanford White would be one of the parties. She objected to my going. My girlfriend then came to the house. She was going, accompanied by her own mother.

"I should not think of letting my daughter go," she said, "unless the people were nice."

The girl explained that the people at the party would be some of the nicest in New York society. The function was a luncheon, and mother consented. She dressed me so carefully for that occasion. I was very expectant and excited. I was hoping it would be at the Waldorf, because I was most anxious to see this famous restaurant. But the cab that carried us off went down Forty-eighth Street and onto West Twenty-fourth Street, and stopped at a dingy, little door. It was rather disappointing after all my dreams of magnificent dining rooms, but there was adventure in it, and my curiosity freed me from any hint of apprehension that I might otherwise have felt. We got out of the cab, and my friend paid and dismissed the man.

The other door opened, apparently by itself, and we went through it, up some stairs, at the head of which another door opened in the same way. It was all delightfully mysterious, and to one who had read many mystery stories, and was steeped in the traditions of conventional melodrama, it was an adventure. Yet I had some qualms, and halfway up the stairs I stopped.

"Where are we going?" I asked.

"It's all right," smiled Edna.

I did not feel it was all right, but I did not wish to appear foolish or to display any of the fear I felt; after all, her mother

33

had vouched for the respectability of the people I was going to meet. We continued our climb. Suddenly a voice above said: "Hullo! Who's there?" The voice was Stanford White's.

He met us at the head of the stairs, and he ushered us into the most gorgeous room I have ever seen. It was Oriental in its design, yet the Orientalism was of the most refined and delicate character. It was hung around with velvet; divans and great billowing cushions were everywhere, tiny little Oriental tables, all the impedimenta of luxury, were displayed on either hand.

Stanford White was a man of exquisite taste. He had ranged the world to furnish this apartment. There was not one object which was garish, commonplace, or out of harmony with the beauty of the furnishing.

It was then that I received my first impression of Stanford White. His size was appalling, and I was not impressed by his looks. The table was laid for luncheon, a table for four, and he was engaged in making me feel at home, in a way peculiarly his own, when another man came in, Reginald Ronalds, as I discovered. There was little preliminary talk; we sat down to table to enjoy a meal ordered by one of the best known of epicures. I had, and have, a very healthy appetite, and lunch was less of a pleasant social function than a very serious business.

I enjoyed that luncheon tremendously, but much more did I enjoy the fun, which was mostly at my expense. For you have to remember that I was still a very young girl—my frocks were short, my hair was down my back—and I was in no sense above the things which delighted girls of my age. I loved the fun at my expense, the irresponsible happiness of that party. I was at the age when I looked forward with considerable interest to the entremets. After lunch was over, Mr. Ronalds went away. He had some business in Wall Street, and I was left alone with White and my girl friend. We sat some time in the apartment, chatting about the various objects we saw upon the walls and the floor, each with some interesting history of its own, and then Mr. White said—

"I've some other rooms upstairs. I think you would like to see them."

We went up another two flights of stairs, and came to the room at the top of the building. My first impression of the room was that extended in the very center was a large velvet chair swinging on two ropes from the ceiling, and above this chair, closer to the ceiling, was hung a big open Japanese umbrella of paper.

"Let me give you a swing," said Stanford White. I got into the chair, and he swung me higher and higher, till I almost touched the umbrella.

"I want to see your feet go through it." He said, swinging me more vigorously; and soon after I accomplished what he desired, for my feet went crashing through the paper cover of the umbrella. It was amusing. I enjoyed it thoroughly. I did not realize that childish fun could have any serious significance. I did not realize that this prepossessing and kindly man could have any other object in view than to amuse me.

After a while he looked at his watch.

"I should like to stay here all day," he said with a smile, "keeping you amused; but unfortunately I am a very busy man."

He glanced round at my companion.

"I want to see you for a moment," he said, and went out with her. In a little time she came back to me. She told me that she had to go to a dentist and that we should go for a little ride in an automobile round Central Park and afterwards I might go with her. It was Mr. White's suggestion that I should do this. He thought that an experienced dentist should see my teeth, and I welcomed the suggestion.

I told mother all about the party and the subsequent visit to the dentist; there was nothing to hide and nothing in the afternoon's experience which seemed in any way out of place, and mother apparently took the same view.

In a few days mother received a letter from him, asking her to call at 160, Fifth Avenue. Poor mother was rather flustered because she did not know at that time whether 160 Fifth Avenue was his home or his office. The interview with him was a very satisfactory one. I think mother must have been impressed by his kindness. He wanted her to take me to a dentist in New York to have all my teeth seen to. It was rather a fad of White's, this teeth-seeing. I realize now the supreme importance of this timely visit to the dentist, and I do not think it so strange as I did at the moment. He had arranged for almost every girl in *Florodora* to be put right by the dentist. Here then, we have a curious sidelight upon the character of the man. His thought for the girls in so important a matter gives one a glimpse of his large benevolence.

I remember, in reading Maurice Hewlett's *Richard Yea-and-Nay*[7], being struck by the mystery of the relationship that existed between old King Henry, his son John, and the woman whom Richard was to marry. There was something very sinister in her comings and goings.

Stanford White had girl friends about which I knew nothing. They may have been innocent agents of his; but their work on his behalf may have been of a less innocent character. Yet for so big a man he was absurdly anxious to keep his friends separate and distinct. I remember once when I saw him at a luncheon at the studio in Twenty-fourth Street there was another girl. It was not the one who had taken me first to his apartment. When he invited me he told me that there would be a young lady there, whom I already knew.

"You must not ask me who it is until you see her and, whatever you do, do not tell that she was with us."

---

[7] *The Life and Death of Richard Yea-and-Nay* was an historical novel by Maurice Henry Hewlett published in 1900.

In many ways his friendship was practical. He sent me a hat and a feather boa along with a red cape on one occasion. It was a present that a man could give to a girl of my age without offence. I was to wear it to a party, and mother made me a new dress especially for the occasion and sent it to the theatre. The evening of the party, a carriage was waiting for me on the other side of Twenty-ninth Street outside of the theatre. A man stepped out from the door of a greengrocer's store opposite from where the carriages were standing, it was Stanford White.

The furtive character of the meeting did not impress me so much then as it does today. He got into the carriage with me and we drove to Madison Square Garden. These little facts have impressed themselves on my memory, because I have so often gone over the circumstances that attended that party, striving, often vainly, to recall all that happened. We talked about nothing in particular. I thought it was curious that he should come to meet me, but his attitude was always kindly and deferential. When we went up the elevator in the tower of Madison Square Garden, we found another girl and another man already there.

It was replica of the other luncheon party. I remember I nibbled chocolate éclairs and drank a glass of champagne. Only once, however, did Stanford White put out a detaining hand when I pushed my glass forward.

"One is quite enough for a little girl," he said. "I want you to be a nice little girl."

"What do you think is a nice little girl?" I asked laughingly.

But he was very serious.

"It is one who doesn't stay up late," he said. "One who goes home to her mother at an early hour."

It seemed rather a dull way of ending the evening, but he escorted me back to the very door of the apartment in the Audubon Hotel, and wakened mother.

Mother and Stanford White were quite good friends. He visited her on several occasions. He was always very courteous in his relationship. Mother was impressed by his anxiety for my welfare. He was so safe a man, so eminently solid, and there was so little that was not nice-spoken about him, that my mother might well be excused for regarding him as a heaven-sent friend of the family, a veritable second father.

And here I may say that though Stanford White was a notorious man in New York, and though there was hardly a man about town who did not know him and of him, there were none who warned me. He was a powerful man, and, in spite of his peculiarities, a very popular man. Men, and women, too, for that matter, are prone to excuse viciousness that wears a pleasant guise, and it requires greater courage to go up against popularity than it does to lead an army in the field.

I find no difficulty in telling the story of Stanford White, and the influence he exercised over my life, unless it is the difficulty of avoiding the melodrama of it.

I want to tell the story as one in whom such physical changes have occurred as to another person.

Sentimentality is as much out of place in an autobiography as it would be in a timetable, and it is more satisfactory to me to get outside myself and regard the big incident in my life from the outsider's point of view without fear, favor, or prejudice.

It is not an easy task I set myself, but it is considerably easier than it would have been a few years ago.

For example, it might be unjust at this moment to explain every action of Stanford White in the light of his subsequent conduct. I have no doubt in my mind that in many of the things he did White was motivated by the purest kindness. Such was the complexity of the man's character that he could at one and the same time be the disinterested patron and the scheming roué.

He had established himself in my mother's good graces, was a frequent visitor at our house and now became suddenly interested in mother's movements.

He displayed a solicitude that took a significant shape. He knew we had friends in Pittsburgh.

"You ought to visit your Pittsburgh friends," he said to mother. "It is never advisable to drop people out of your life. Why don't you run over to Pittsburgh and see them?"

Mother was not very enthusiastic.

"That would mean leaving Evelyn alone in New York," she said, coming at once to the very heart of the matter.

Mr. White smiled.

"I am here," he said. "She can hardly be alone when I am around to look after her."

The plan fell through, but only for a while. His visits became more frequent, and he brought the project up again. I was not present at every interview, so I am not in a position to reproduce the arguments he employed.

Once he agreed with mother within my hearing.

"I admit," he said, "that but for my presence it would be dangerous to leave an attractive girl alone in New York, but the argument does not hold good any more."

Mother thought the world of Stanford White. He was such a proud man, so kind, so thoughtful, and, above all things, so safe. For I had given her a very faithful account of the parties to which I had been with Mr. White, and there could be no doubt that those parties were beautifully conducted and the attitude of everybody concerned was proper and decorous.

Eventually mother decided on the trip, and Stanford White secured facilities that enabled her to make the journey without expense to herself. Before she went I had promised that in her absence I would not go out with any other person that White.

That promise I kept.

The morning after she had left I had a phone message from him asking me to come to a studio where I was to have some photographs taken. It was early in the morning, and by ten o'clock I was dressed and on my way to the studio in Twenty-second Street. There were two photographers present, and again the proceedings were such as I could find no fault with.

I posed for hours on end, wearing among other things the most gorgeous of Japanese kimonos, which Mr. White told me, had been brought from Hong Kong especially for me. It was a tiring business, but it was over at last, and Mr. White had luncheon for me with that "one glass of champagne and no more" that so emphasized the care he displayed in shaping my conduct.

I mark these visits because they were important to me. Each visit represented an advance in the friendliness of our relationship, each visit make me more and more dependent upon his honor and his integrity.

It was on the night following my visit to the studio that Stanford White dropped the mask of disinterested patronage.

There is a type of person that peeps with insatiable curiosity at anything that is tagged "private."

It has an irresistible temptation to open any letter, pass through any door and unearth any plan that bears that label. Curiosity is the besetting virtue of an age that has come to maturity by finding out things for itself. There are episodes in our lives that we would desire to forget if we could only avoid that one moment of publicity which make the public as wise as we are. Let that one moment come and one's memory is no longer one's own. It is no longer in your discretion to remember or forget. We have taken to ourselves, willy-nilly, a remembrance that is a once a conscience and an index.

A jealously guarded secret may be pinhead of memory but it swells to fill the world. In every newspaper office it is indexed, and tabulated in the dusty files of official records and in the minds of those who love the secrets of others. It is a frightening experience to hear a thought that you have never given even words babbled aloud in the street. It takes on a new horror; it garnishes memory with a new shame. It sets you frantically anxious to amend, to contradict, to correct. Your little secret is everybody's secret now. It has gained in importance, has been twisted in detail until it is like nothing you ever knew.

If all the stories of Stanford White, myself, Harry Thaw, and other people who figured so largely in my life are to be stripped of their excrescences and brought down to the bareness and the cleanness of truth, I must in this story speak about that which I would rather forget.

# CHAPTER IV
# HOW RUIN CAME

I write this chapter a little cold-bloodily. I must do that, or I should not write it at all. I must tell all that is to be told, because around this night that I will describe circled the tragedy that destroyed the life of one man, helped to undermine the reason of another, and dragged me into the fierce light of publicity and criticism, an experience that could otherwise have been avoided.

In the course of the trial, to which I shall make reference later, the prosecuting attorney, speaking under stress of some emotion, said there was no one to speak for Mr. White save himself. That is not true. I would speak of White with as great a charity as any lawyer. I can more easily find explanation for his character than those who did not know him as well as I. In the balance between the living and the dead, the dead have suffered for their acts, and the living may still be suffering, the weight of prejudice most favors the living, for the dead are asleep, and are unconscious of puerile criticism.

Stanford White was a member of a small clique of men who had vicious tendencies. I am not speaking disparagingly when I use the word "vicious." I am merely stating what I think to be an obvious fact. If he had only had a weakness for drunkenness, if he had been a spendthrift, or guilty of some crime that made him amenable to the laws of the land, if, in fact, he had committed any act that had no effect upon my career or upon my life, I would speak just as dispassionately.

Nature is very cruel; it is merciless and remorseless. The instruments of the great scheme, their sufferings, their terrors, are as nothing. All that counts is that certain laws should be obeyed, certain instincts fulfilled, and if civilization has overlaid us with delicacies and refinements, nature continues on just as though social laws had no existence.

The strong are as cruel to the weak as ever they had been, and there are brutalities that are as far outside the governing laws now as ever.

I went to the establishment at Twenty-fourth Street that night a child with no knowledge of the big and stunning facts of life other than any other child has, and if you say to me, "How is it possible that you could live in such an atmosphere as you did, surrounded by significant evidences as you were that the world was less than the idyllic place you pretend, and still be innocent?" I reply that there is an innocence that finds for evident evil an innocent explanation.

I remember that I was hungry and the supper he offered me was acceptable, and the comfort of the place was pleasing. Think of this cozy room, with its shaded lights, its thick carpets, its divans, its rare objects of art. There was no jarring note in the composition, no picture that offended or any touch of color that irritated. Nor to my eyes was there any note of decadence that might cause the slightest uneasiness; a pleasant meal with a pleasant man, a sense of security and well-being — that is my memory of that night.

My mother went out of town. I was alone in New York, under the guardianship of Stanford White. I was utterly and entirely at his mercy. He dominated me by his kindness and by his authority. He abused the sacred trust that had been put into his hands; nothing else matters.

It was the night following my visit to the photographer that I went to dine with White. He had sent me a note asking me to one of his parties, and I went without any fear of consequences to the Twenty-fourth Street house. Young people very easily get familiar with the ways of folk, and when I walked into the room where White was it was without hesitation, and perhaps with something of a proprietorial air, since I had come to regard him as being bound to me by some vague relationship. The table was laid, but only White was waiting.

"Where are the rest of the people?" I asked, a little astonished.

Stanford White was all apologies.

"Isn't it too bad?" he protested. "These people had turned us down."

I was terribly disappointed, because the people were as interesting as the dinner, and he must have seen my look of disappointment.

"You're not worried about them, are you?" he asked.

I nodded.

"Yes, I am," I said. "I am very sorry, for there will be no party now."

I suppose I showed my disappointment very clearly.

"Never mind," he said, "we will eat alone."

He drew back a chair from the table and we sat down. It was one of those comfortable little meals when nothing of importance happened. We just talked and talked, and since he was one of the most interesting men in New York I was not bored. He left me alone for a little while after supper and I made preparations for going home. He came back in a very short time.

"You're not going?" he said.

Some instinct must have warned me, for it was not usual for me to go home so early.

"Stay," he pleaded, "there is a lot in this house you have never seen, and it will amuse you."

He talked about the furnishing of the place. He had brought this article from Venice, that from London, that from China.

"I have another room upstairs that you have not seen," he said, and he led the way up a tiny flight of stairs that I had not hitherto known existed.

"I want you to see all my beautiful home," he said.

We came into a back studio that I had not seen before. It was a bedroom and very small, but furnished with exquisite taste. There were pictures on the walls. I was looking at the picture over the mantel, a very beautiful one that attracted my attention. I sat down at a tiny, little table. There was a bottle of champagne on it, a small bottle and one glass. Stanford White picked up the bottle and poured the champagne into the glass until it was full. My eyes were drawn back to the picture and he told me what it was and told me to finish the champagne. The champagne was bitter and funny-tasting, and I didn't care for it much. Then a pounding began in my ears and the whole room began to go around and everything went black.

When I woke up, all my clothes were pulled off me. I was in bed. I sat up and I started to scream. Stanford got up and put on one of his kimonos, the kimono had been laying on a chair. I moved up and pulled some covers over me. There were mirrors all around the bed; mirrors on the sides of the wall and on the top. I looked down and saw blotches of blood on the sheets. I began to scream.

He came over and asked me to keep quiet.

"It's all over, it's all over," he said.

He brought a kimono over to me and went out of the room. I don't remember how I got my clothes on. I do remember that Stanford took me home.

I recollect sitting on a chair by the window of my room and watching the dawn come up over the great city.

I sat cramped and shivering, thinking and, thinking. And in this chair Stanford White found me when he called in the morning.

I felt nothing, neither repulsion nor hate. He was a strange being to me; an aspect of life revealed in a flash and changing all my perspectives.

And here he was, pleading with me, kneeling on the floor by my side, kissing the hem of my gown in an extravagance of remorse, in that he did me the greatest wrong of all; for to excuse himself he blackened all humanity to one drab and sordid hue.

Everybody was bad; everybody was evil. Evil was the basis of life.

So he ran on.

That woman was bad—that man was vicious. He mentioned names easily. Society people, stage people, every rank and class of society, they were all steeped in evil. He was no worse than other men, a little better by his own showing. He illustrated his argument with stories.

There was one sin that the entire world would recognize as such—the sin of being found out—that was unforgivable. You must just go along as if nothing had happened and people would respect you.

And it was a terrible thing to talk. A girl must never talk; she must just keep things locked up in her bosom and confide in nobody. It was unpardonable to chatter—look at Miss—. If she hadn't told things about people she would have been in a splendid position. "Don't talk, Evelyn—tell nobody, and nobody will know."

Most important of all, I must not tell my mother. To tell one's mother things meant all the world knowing. Mothers never kept things to themselves.

So he went on, sometimes pleading, sometimes covertly menacing, and I listened, dazed and bewildered, as all the fair fabrics of my faith crumbled into dust. He was convincing to a point and that point was the instinct that is implanted in every heart—the scale that weights good and evil. He was older and so much wiser and cleverer—but I was so young.

No human soul can stand alone. Cut out the faith and the trust and you must substitute something for it to lean upon. I listened and disbelieved and trusted. I had to build up a new faith, and needed scaffolding, a shell from whence to work. I never wholly accepted Stanford White's creed, it was too rotten a foundation to build any life upon, but from a raging sea, even quicksand seems solid foothold to the wrecked mariner, and quicksand served until I reached firm earth.

I cannot remember now whether I knew Harry Thaw before the events recorded in the last chapter. I used to receive at the theatre letters from a very persistent correspondent, asking me out to lunch. They were written under an assumed name and were evidently from a man of some refinement. Once they came accompanied by some money, which I sent back. As in the case of White, my actual meeting with Harry was through the instrumentality of a girl friend.

My first impression of Mr. Thaw was an unpleasant one. I met a man whose face attracted and at the same time repelled me. There was a curious look in his eyes, a sinister brutality about the mouth that had an unpleasant effect upon me. Our first meeting—it was at a restaurant, and, as I say, I had the society of another girl—was made up of a fairly harmless quarrel between him and myself, the subject being the beauty of member of the chorus. Harry Thaw spoke unkindly of her and I remembered I defended her. I left him with the sense of relief one secures when one get through with a disagreeable person.

I had no desire to meet him again. I was not very much interested, if the truth be told, he was only a pleasant young man who paid me the compliment of admiring me from the other side of the footlights.

He was not, of course, the only person who wrote me letters expressing a wish to make my acquaintance. A girl on the stage receives such letters in shoals from all sorts of people— good, bad, and indifferent—and when I had met him I thought merely that his curiosity was satisfied and that was an end of it.

But he was indeed persistent. He pursued me with his harmless attentions. It was after another such party to which I had been invited, and the invitation to which I had accepted, that he revealed himself to me. We had come back from the restaurant and I was entering the theatre, when all of a sudden he said, with almost dramatic earnestness: "I am not—" (the man whose name he had given); "I am Harry Thaw, of Pittsburgh!"

I looked at him with some amusement. He was so earnest; there was such a trembling pride in his voice; a disguised Napoleon revealing himself to a near-sighted veteran could not have made the revelation with greater aplomb.

I do not know what he expected me to do.

I had an uncanny feeling that I should stagger back, or should turn pale, or should do something. I do not say this unkindly, but it struck me as funny at the time and so very like Harry. Indeed, so characteristic was it that I do not think I ever knew him much better at any subsequent time than I did at that moment.

I contented myself by saying, "Indeed!" There seemed little else to say. He was "Harry Thaw, of Pittsburgh"—that was enough. In one minute he had told me the full story of his condescension, the explanation of those letters written under a *nom de plume*. Harry Thaw, of Pittsburgh, was somebody.

It irritated and amused me, this attitude of his. But even a pose, so long as it is consistently upheld, is impressive. Men who acclaim their own importance persistently and with no sign of hesitation as to their own conviction on the subject cease to be nobodies and become some bodies. And the egotism which prompted Harry's sentence and which appeared in all his dealings with the remainder of humanity at once fascinated and annoyed.

Harry Thaw was an earnest young man. There was a side of him that was rather terrible, as you will learn. He was very earnest, no philanderer, no light lover, even in his infidelities he was absorbed and sincere. Such matters were serious propositions, presenting aspects that would not occur to the normal man.

When his mind took that turn he played at reformer with all the enthusiasm of a Savonarola.[8] He was very earnest about himself. He took Harry Thaw and his position in life very seriously. It has always been a wonderful thing to me that he has not written the story of his life. Perhaps it is because he does not possess the sense of humor that makes such a performance possible.

He took his position seriously: his world value too seriously. Like man egotists there was a very gentle and kind side to him. It would be an ungracious thing to say that such gentleness and sweetness were part of his egotism. Let me put all his generosity to his credit, for it was only his arrogance of thought and action that was to bring about his downfall.

His persistence was of a fine order. He never left me alone; he was everlastingly following me. He was not offensive, nor was his attitude one to which I could take any exception. In course of time, I grew to like him and to regard him as a dear and reliable friend. He introduced me to his mother and became acquainted with my own mother, and the course of our friendship ran fairly smooth.

It was long after the events that I have described in a previous chapter that he became a factor in my life. The miserable friendship between Stanford White and myself was in progress. Faithful to my promise I had told nobody. I had accepted his conception of life with a dull sense of helplessness. Here was a phase of humanity that I could not change, here was a strong stream running which I could not breast. I must go with the stream if I would find my bearings.

An enormous cataclysm that comes to a young life leaves little impression on the spirit of the child. Doctors say that

---

[8] Girolamo Savonarola was an Italian Dominican priest and, briefly, ruler of Florence, who was known for religious reformation during the fifteenth century.

children who lose their limbs in accidents come to maturity with a sense of having been born as they are, without any recollection of previously having been better equipped for the battle of life. Young people who lose their parents at my age have the greatest difficulty in retaining a memory of those parents, however kindly, and however apparently indispensable they may have been in their lifetime. It may seem a shocking thing that I did not become melancholic, or so depressed as to take no interest in life, but a healthy child—and I was only sixteen, be it remembered—abhors bad memories and all the gloomy morbid machinery of introspection. I found myself almost as I had been before that night, with interests as keen, with as poignant a sense of humor as ever, though a change had come to me and though my angle of vision had altered.

There was one of my frolics that alarmed White. I believe that he was genuinely fond of me, and that he took an unselfish pleasure in making my life brighter. He arranged holidays for me, saw that I should not suffer from lack of work, and generally was good and kind. But an all night party of which I was a member irked him.

I must go to school, he said; I was not fit for the work I was doing; I must fit myself for life, as I would find it.

It was a dismal prospect for me, to be lifted out of the light and glitter of Broadway to the quiet and peaceful dullness of a convent school, and it did not appeal to me. But he and my mother insisted, and off to school I was packed.

It was an amusing experience, because Mr. White had made laborious arrangements that my association with the stage should not be mentioned, but it leaked out somehow.

I found myself among these girls as something of a heroine.

I was a real live actress transplanted into their midst. We used to have little plays and make up with some homemade cosmetics. Toothpowder laid on with a piece of wadding was and excellent substitute for *poudre de riz,*[9] and I shudder when I think of the substitutes we employed for rouge and lip salve.

From time to time Mr. White came down to see me, and at other times I went to New York to see him. Exactly what would have happened had I not been seized with an attack of appendicitis I do not know. The attack was so sudden that it was necessary for the doctors who were called in to operate on me in the school, and while I was there Mr. Thaw was a frequent visitor. During the operation itself Harry and my mother walked up and down the garden outside discussing my future, though there seemed at the moment to be little future for me.

Mr. Thaw seemed absorbed in my welfare so far as my health and happiness were concerned.

"Evelyn will never recuperate unless she goes for a voyage," he told my mother, "and we must get her to Europe."

I needed little persuasion to explore the wonderful new world that was awaiting me beyond the seas. Our plans were made and we sailed, Mr. Thaw, my mother and myself, to Europe. The voyage made all the difference to me. I began to pick up health and strength the moment we sailed. Harry was most good and attentive. I began to lose the heavy sense of oppression that had weighed on me during the months I was at school. The influence of Stanford White grew smaller; a new life was opening before me. Harry had proposed to me before we sailed. I think he proposed twice, but on both occasions I had refused him. I realized I could not marry any man unless he knew everything there was to be known about me. This was a matter of common honesty, and I take no credit for desiring to be frank and above-board with my future husband.

For the moment I had no wish to tell him. I was quite happy in the enjoyment of the present, quite willing to let the past slip from memory and the future take care of itself.

---

[9] Rice powder or dust.

# CHAPTER V
# WITH HARRY THAW

Some women have a conscience, some have a sense of self-preservation; they frequently exist together, but most often one does duty for the other. Conscience is an uneasy desire for frank dealing, and I suppose it was a suppressed conscience that made me sweep aside what would have been a very advantageous offer. Had Thaw been any other kind of man, he might have been satisfied to let matters slide, to take such happiness as the gods gave him in the way their chosen instruments choose to offer it.

But he was, as I say, persistent. He wanted to marry. Nothing else, nothing less would satisfy him. We were the best of friends in London, though it was in London that I first had some idea of his perversity. A brutal assault committed upon a boy at one of the leading hotels, a flogging that was unjustifiable and wicked, almost ruined Harry, and it cost him 5000 dollars to square the matter. The story, as I have heard it, was that Harry put a lot of money upon a table, and watched behind a screen when a boy, who had been summoned to the room, came in.

The temptation of the money was irresistible, and the boy took two gold coins. Immediately Harry pounced upon him, took him to the bathroom, and flogged him so terribly that the poor child had to go home.

A doctor was called in, and eventually a lawyer. There can be no doubt that Harry's objective in laying a trap for a boy who had shown no disposition to steal was to administer a flogging—a practice that in some way seemed to gratify him.

Contrast this side of his character with the scene that followed when mother had gone back to America and Harry and I were alone in Paris. He came into my suite one night. He said he wanted to speak to me. I thought he looked haggard and worried, and I closed the door and invited him in.

Without any preliminary he came to the point.

"I want you to marry me," he said.

He was as dogged and as persistent as ever. There was no fending him off with excuses, with reasons or with explanations as to why marriage was not desirable. I knew in an instant that now he must know the truth, must take his answer for good or evil.

"I cannot marry you," I said.

"Why not?"

"Because —"

"Do you not love me?"

I nodded.

"Then why —?" he repeated.

"Because —" I said slowly.

He walked toward me and laid his hand on my shoulder, looking straight into my eyes.

"Is it because of Stanford White?" he asked; and I nodded again.

I hesitated a moment.

"Sit down over there and I will tell you everything."

It was a story that was difficult to tell. But it had to be done. Very slowly, very deliberately, making no excuse for myself, giving no place to prejudice against White, I told him all that had happened from the very beginning.

He sat in silence for a while, his hands shaking, his face ghastly; then he rose and walked up and down the room, his shaking hands gesticulating as he muttered.

Then when I reached the climax of the story he sat down suddenly, burying his face in his hands, and burst into tears.

You saw all that was best in Harry Thaw then, all the finer sides of him, all the womanliness in him, all the Quixote that was in his composition.

He sat there sobbing "Poor child! Poor child!"

The relationship between Mr. Thaw and myself at that time was one of complete sympathy. There had been some unpleasantness in London. Mother had returned to the States as a result of a disagreement, and Mr. Thaw, who saw turreted castles in every windmill and armies in every flock of sheep, was prepared to repudiate the suggestion that he had kidnapped me.

Here is a letter he wrote to Mr. Longfellow, his attorney. It deals with my mother. "She states that I have kidnapped her daughter. Before she lands she will know that I have done the best I could." That he had the most extraordinary ideas may be gathered from one extract.

"Telephone Mrs. Nesbit," he instructs, "but not in your own name, and ask her if she saw Thaw abroad. As soon as she answers hang up the receiver."

It was here that he adopted the role of reformer. He began writing letters to the vigilance societies exposing White.

You might think very well indeed of Harry Thaw, his generosity, his boyish enthusiasm for the cause he had suddenly espoused, and there is no reason why he should not have all the credit that is due to him for his impressive championing of righteousness; but it has to be remembered that Thaw himself was something of a moral pervert. Of his flogging propensities there is no need to tell. He was given to practices that are not pleasant to relate. On one occasion, as I was told, he had amused himself by pouring boiling hot water over a girl in a bath; and on another occasion he had flogged a young girl who had been strapped to a bed-post. Such a mixture of good and evil could hardly be found without mental derangement. • My own view is, that at that time the melancholia that dominated him had begun to take firm hold.

I sailed to New York before him with my marriage practically arranged for, and he followed a short time after.

All this time Harry was in correspondence with his mother. She was in many ways a remarkable woman, and enjoyed the confidence of her children. He took his intentions very seriously, and was not inclined to accept any advice that might be offered.

He told her about Stanford White, and he had an opportunity of seeing how the story affected her when he returned to America. He was prone to exaggerate the virtues of his friends and the failings of those he regarded as his enemies. He spoke of me as having a beautiful mind. Perhaps healthy would have been a better word, for I had come to the time when I saw things in their true proportions.

In justice to Mrs. Thaw, it must be said that she did everything that she could do to prevent the marriage. She acted, as any mother would have done who thought she saw a *misalliance*. For the Thaws, though of no great social standing, were extremely rich, and I, though of good birth, was extremely poor; the society in Pittsburgh is governed by the initials that indicate the Almighty dollar.

When she did agree to the marriage it was on the understanding that my past should be a closed book. I did not know this till later. I certainly had no objection to the condition. Nobody desired more earnestly to close my past: it needed less closure than obliteration, and unfortunately in life even the desire of a Pittsburgh millionaire does not altogether influence the recording angel to the employment of an eraser.

I do not believe that Mrs. Thaw was filled with sympathy for me. I certainly had no great sympathy for her. I never regarded Mrs. Thaw as an archangel because she was so magnanimous as to forgive a chorus girl for taking her favorite son. For the Thaws had married well. They had an earl in the family and a Carnegie. Harry Thaw's qualities might have added further luster to the brand new escutcheon.

I have sympathy for Mrs. Thaw in this respect. The end of it was that after much discussion, after many heartaches, after great searching of conscience and of soul—not on my part, be it noted—I was married to Harry Thaw in a Presbyterian church, into a Presbyterian circle, and sentenced in the terms of my marriage vow to live forthwith in the charmed circle of a Presbyterian home.

The Pittsburgh home was never a home for me.

Harry and I occupied a wing and we met the family at luncheon and dinner.

I have observed that relations by marriage are seldom in sympathy, and I cannot regard my own particular case as being extraordinary. The Thaws were under some disadvantage with me, and to an extent I fully understood their dilemma. Their son had taken for a wife an actress—call me a chorus girl, if you like; it makes very little difference what label you stick. Had they been particularly well-bred, had they been intellectually and socially among the gods, I should have been surprised had they patronized me, but I should have understood. I should have been surprised because your well-bred American is the truest type of nobleman the world offers. But on the point of view of caste, I had some slight advantage. The Thaws had risen on very unsolid foundations. They had become financial aristocrats in a night, and aristocracy at best is a slow-growing plant and requires at least fifty years' cultivation. It was irritating for these strict souls to have a chorus girl in the family, and her "beautiful mind" was little compensation for her association with the stage. But still less pleasant, was to have around a chorus girl who was, at times, obviously bored.

It would sound priggish to speak of the family as moving on a lower intellectual plane; rather let me say, that it moved on a different plane, the plane of materialism that finds a joy in the little things that do not matter—the appearance of a new minister, the comforts of a pew, the profits of a church bazaar—

excellent and admirable characters, but none designed to keep my thoughts busy.

Those dinners!  Those ministers who came in benign and stately procession!   And last, but not least, those ministers' wives!  They were good women; they invariably acted with the best of intentions; they said things with a monotony and a sameness that led me to suppose that there existed somewhere in America a school for ministers' wives where they were taught to say the same things in identical terms.

At first they interested me because they were a type with which I was not familiar.  I thought their views on life cute and novel—indeed, I could not get it out of my head that these views were part of a pose; but afterwards, I found that they were in earnest and that they believed in themselves, that their atrocious taste in dress was not a design but an accident, that their terrible triteness was a part of them.  Right here I say that I am not sneering at ministers' wives because they are ministers' wives.  I don't think I met the best of them.  I should be sorry to think I met the most intelligent of them.  They were products of formalism, victims of tight, iron-bound ritualism and nonconformity.  Their attitude towards me was an attitude of forgiveness and charity.  They hoped for the best.

It was an understood thing that my past was dead.  Mrs. Thaw had demanded that it should be forgotten.  Nobody ever referred to my stage days, but I lived in an atmosphere of grim consciousness:   I was a sinner whose name with great advantage might be tacked on the end of a list of distant relations at prayer time.  I think there must have been a mighty lot of praying for me behind my back, and I did some pretty earnest praying on my own account.  My prayers took the shape of a request that I might have patience to bear the burden of my spiritual friends.

The Thaw house did not cheer me.  It was not a bright house.  Harry was the only member of the family who had any taste in either decoration or furnishing.  He brought into the house the only pictures that were worth looking at, and he represented the sole artistic side of the family.

He was, I remember, extremely patient and tactful in those days, and whenever it was possible he shielded me from such oblique attacks as came my way. He took some interest in Church work and was not so readily bored with the trivialities of the profession as I, and it was a standing wonder to me — and a cause for admiration — to hear him enter so heartily into the details of an organ fund or the work of this guild or the other.

I confess I did not understand, nor do I understand now, a certain type of Christian. There was a clergyman who was a frequent visitor to the house, who had been associated with my marriage. He was very nice, a very fair specimen of Christianity. One morning, when we were sitting in the front of the house, a dog of mine came along, and in its light-hearted fashion jumped upon the knees of the reverend gentleman. His reward was a kick that sent the poor dog flying.

I always tried to behave myself with that decorum that the position called for, but here was an instance that roused all the latent devil in me, and, to the horror and consternation of all the Thaws present, I rose and in such violent language as I could summon to my command, spoke very freely. It was not perhaps a tactful thing to do, but I am a great lover of animals.

I do not think it is peculiar to Pittsburgh society that there are cliques of people whose whole lives are bound up in the solely business side of Church work. I have had a hint of such interest elsewhere. But in Pittsburgh, I was brought daily into contact with the very center of the movement. There are people, it seems, who take the same interest in religion that the public does in baseball. They are the religious fans that shout their side on without doing so much as lift a club themselves. Then there is the committee that engages, criticizes, and organizes the players, knows the rules by heart, exploits the game and understands its technique from A to Z. They know the rules of the game without exerting themselves to play it;

they have its argot and its terminology at their fingertips. "Grace," "salvation," "light," "redemption" comes glibly. They use beautiful words in such a manner as to strip their beauty and leave them just meaningless skeletons of speech; they employ phrases which spoken from the soul would have moved men and women to tears, but as uttered, are but the dry husks of thought.

I give all credit to the Thaw family for desiring to make me something different from what I was, but with the best intentions in the world they could do no more than what they did, because human nature is so constituted that temperament is not amenable to tuition. And character is as little susceptible to reorganization as is the human body. Indeed, while you may improve the latter by systems of training, it is the same old body, and while in a plastic nature you may bring character to a certain state of advancement, nothing short of a miracle can amend it so that it may be completely uniform with its environment. It is neither credible nor discreditable to me that I could not mix in the society in which I found myself, I moved on another plane from that occupied by the people with whom I was daily brought into contact. The parties, the receptions, the At-homes, they all bored me.

I remember one day escaping from a particularly dull function and making my way to the garden at the back of the house. There were some rat-holes in an outhouse that appealed to me. There was a gardener who had some idea of sport, and a garden hose to flush the rodent from his lair. Here Mrs. Thaw found me, oblivious of the joys that the reception offered. Such an incident, small as it was, I number among my happy landmarks of the life I spent in the Thaw establishment.

Mrs. Thaw was a stickler for propriety. No aristocrat of ancient lineage could have been stricter than she was.

I was not altogether a success, though I tried very hard to conform to the demands made upon me.

When I returned from Europe, I had again seen White, though only for a few minutes. He had not approved of my trip to Europe, and was bitterly angry that Harry should have taken me away. Nevertheless, he seemed to be reconciled to my departure, for he had given me a letter of credit if I needed it. I had been ill, the trip was in the nature of a recuperative journey, and Stanford White was sufficiently unselfish to wish for my complete recovery. He had not perhaps realized the part that Harry Thaw was playing, nor had he any idea that it was due to Harry's kindness and generosity that I was able to go to Europe at all. (I may say in parenthesis that the letter of credit he gave me was never employed.)

White and Harry were not good friends. This did not date from my acquaintance with Harry. There was an antagonism of long standing, though it did not reach a bitter phase till later.

They knew one another, just as men who move in a certain set know one another. The situation became more critical when I returned from Europe. I began to learn things about Harry that I had not known before. Indeed, to my astonishment I found that Harry's peculiarities were public property. One man after another told me things about him that I had never expected: he took morphine; he was crazy.

White supported all this talk. He was very vehement in his indictment of Harry's iniquities. He was a little frightened, too, I think, and went to great pains to remove any influence that he may have had upon me. He even went so far as to take me to the office of Abe Hummel, the lawyer, to show or read to me the portion of a document, part of a suit that had been instituted against Thaw by somebody he had wronged.

I was very dispirited, because I never thought of Harry as a blackguard, as these statements made him out to be, and when Harry returned to America a month after myself it was to find me changed.

I made no secret of the cause. I told him the first time I saw him. I was so distressed that I would not see him alone when he came to the Hotel Navarre, and he brought a man with him.

I shall always remember that interview. I was sitting on a trunk in my room when he came in and walked over and took my hand and sat beside me.

"What is wrong with you, Evelyn?" he asked quietly.

I shook my head. "I don't know what to say to you," I said in distress. "I have heard such dreadful things about you, such dreadful things that I feel I can never speak to you again."

For I was genuinely fond of Harry by this time, and the stories affected me to an extraordinary degree, and they were not nice stories. They placed him among the blackest of humanity. I had had my faith so shaken once, and I hardly suspected how dependent I was upon this new influence that had come into my life.

I told him everything, and he shook his head.

"Poor little Evelyn," he said, laying his hand on my shoulder, "they had been lying to you."

I told him; too, of Stanford White, and that he had taken me to Abe Hummel's office, and showed me the papers in the suit.

"Blackmail," said Harry promptly.

I said very little more. He was so sincere, and showed such a depth of feeling that I felt I had wronged him.

"If you want to believe these things you may," he said, and kissed my hand at parting.

He was still solicitous for my welfare. He watched my health as tenderly as a woman. He used every subterfuge to get back to my good graces. It was at a dinner to which I had gone with a girl that the final reconciliation took place.

I was preparing then to play in a piece called *The Girl from Dixie*. I think it was going to open that night, or it was a dress rehearsal, I don't exactly remember which. Thaw thought I was looking ill, and probably I was. He didn't want me to go into the play. He made all sorts of impossible offers, including one to pay me any salary I was receiving, if for the sake of my health I would abandon the stage. But I had to go. I had no other means of livelihood, and I could not accept all that his generosity prompted.

I have said that this was point of reconciliation, but our relationship was so strange that it is difficult exactly to fix upon the time when our reconciliation was brought about. I met him again at dinner, and again I told him, though with some reluctance, of the stories I had heard.

Harry took the matter seriously.

"The man who told you these stories," he said, "is a friend of Stanford White's. You've known me now for some time, you have seen me under all circumstances, and you may have a reason for believing such dreadful stories about me. If I take morphine," he said with a laugh, "what symptoms can you see? That sort of thing is not done with impunity. It leaves some mark upon a man's face and upon his manner."

Later on, the man who told me the first story contradicted himself, and laughed when I reminded him of the fact. He was confused, and blurted out the truth. "Oh, I did not think you would believe that," he said, and admitted that he had been told to tell the story by somebody. Who that somebody was, is not difficult for me to guess.

For, remember that Harry had never told me a lie, and that beyond certain eccentricities that I had noticed, there was nothing to suggest to me the abnormalities that undoubtedly existed.

These stories, I found afterward, had their foundations in truth, though they had been exaggerated and the details given all wrong, but just as I had believed *in toto*, so I rejected *in toto*, neither of which was a wise proceeding.

63

# CHAPTER VI
# THE MURDER

I can see now how the quarrel began between the two men—the quarrel that was to culminate in White's death.

I told Harry, I had spoken with White since my return, and then and there explained all that had led to our disagreement.

I spoke with White after my return from Europe. I was driving down Fifth Avenue one day in a hansom with my maid when we passed Mr. White, and I heard him exclaim, "Oh, look at Evelyn!"

A few days later I was called to the telephone, and it was White who answered.

"My! But it is good to hear your voice again!" he answered.

He went on to say that he had wanted to come and see me. I told him that I could not possibly see him. He then said it was very important that I should see him, as he had had much trouble with my family and must see me.

I asked if my mother was ill.

He replied that it was a matter of life and death, but he could not tell me over the telephone.

So he came to see me at the Hotel Savoy. He asked me what was the matter. I told him to sit down, and asked again if my mother was ill. He had tried to kiss me, but I would not let him. He said my mother wasn't ill, and then began at once to talk about Mr. Thaw.

He stated that he had learned from various actresses that I had been in Europe with Harry.

Presently he told me that Harry took morphine, and asked why I went around with such a man, remarking that he was not even a gentleman, and that I must have nothing more to do with him. After that he came constantly to see me. He also sent people who told me stories about Harry.

65

"These stories so worried me that I could not sleep." I said to Harry. "I got very nervous, for I knew that you were coming over, and I did not want to see you."

One day White telephoned that he was going to send a carriage, and that I was to come to Broadway, Nineteenth Street.

I did so. He got into the carriage, and said he was taking me to see Abe Hummel, the greatest lawyer in New York, who would protect me from Thaw. He said I was not to be afraid of Hummel. When we got to Hummel's office, White went away.

Hummel's office walls were covered with photographs of actresses, with writing on them. He asked me how I came to go to Europe with Harry, and I replied, "I didn't. I went with my mother and Thaw followed us."

The doctor had told me I could not dance for a year, so I allowed myself that holiday. Hummel had asked me all about the places I had gone to with Harry, and I told him all I could remember.

He said that I was a minor and that Harry should have been more careful. He then stated that he had a case in the office against Thaw and it was about a woman. The case was a very bad one.

"He told me you were a very bad man, and that above all things, I must be protected from you."

White, who had meanwhile returned, then said that what he wanted was to get Harry out of New York, and keep him out of it. They asked me if I had gone to Europe of my own accord, and I said "Certainly." I explained that I had remained in Europe after my mother left because I had quarreled with her, and could not dance for a year, and could not do anything else, and that I liked Mr. Thaw very much,.

"Nevertheless," said Hummel, "you are a minor, and he should not have taken you away from your mother."

"He didn't take me away." I said.

66

White declared that strong measures must be taken to keep Mr. Thaw out of New York, and to protect me, and that I must help in every way I could and leave everything in Hummel's hands.

They sent for a stenographer, and the lawyer said I must not interrupt what he was about to say. I was very nervous and excited, and I think I began to cry.

Then they began to dictate and put in a lot of stuff to the effect that Harry had carried me away against my will.

I started to interrupt, but the lawyer put up his hands and stopped me.

Several days later, Hummel called me on the telephone, and asked it I had any letters from Thaw. I said I had, but I could not see that it had anything to do with him. White also called me up and said if I was not willing to help them in every way they not protect me from Thaw. He added that I must do just what Hummel said.

So I bound the letters up in a bundle and took them down to Hummel's office. He said he did not want to read them, and did not care what they contained. He asked, however, if they were love letters, and I said, "Yes." Hummel told me he just wanted to hold them over Thaw's head.

He then sealed them up in a big envelope. He explained that he did not care anything about them. Then he asked me why I did not sue Harry for breach of promise. I said that was absurd, for if there was any breach of promise it was on my part.

I told Harry all this, and he was eager for more.

He asked me if I had signed anything at Hummel's office, and I said I had not.

"That's funny," said Harry thoughtfully. "If they want to cause trouble, you must have signed something?"

The quarrel became more and more intense. Each man suspected the other of some movement to his discredit. It did not end with my marriage.

Whatever was taboo as to my past did not extend to Harry and myself. He spoke of it again and again; he woke me up in the middle of the night sobbing and demanding from me details that I was loath to give. It was so completely an obsession that I began to fear for his reason and reproach myself for ever having married him. It was never absent from his mind, and although very little more happened between the two men, it culminated disastrously on the 25th of June 1906.

It must be remembered, although I had no warning of Harry's intention, I had lived so much in this atmosphere of hate that I had no doubt as to the condition of his mind. I was satisfied, however, that things would never come to a climax. There was no reason why the two men should meet; indeed, so far as I know, they never did after my marriage.

But Harry had taken this question of White's evil influence upon the young with terrible earnestness. He imagined his life was in danger because of the work he was doing in connection with the vigilance societies and the exposures he had made to those societies of the happenings in White's flat. Because of this fancy of his he was advised to carry a revolver. This I knew, but I was not aware that he was armed when we went out to dinner on that fatal night.

We went to the Café Martin, Mr. Truxton Beale and Mr. McCaleb with us. It was an ordinary dinner party, rather quiet, if anything. We sat on the Twenty-sixth side of the dining room, arriving about eight o'clock in an open motorcar from Sherry's.

We were an hour at dinner, and it was there that I saw Stanford White. He came in from the Fifth Avenue entrance, and went out on the balcony. He came back again from the balcony and went out by the door through which he had entered. He stayed about an hour. All this impressed itself upon me. He was an unexpected vision. Perhaps, too, something of Harry's fear for his safety had been imbued in me, and I took a distorted view of things. At any rate I borrowed a pencil and wrote on a slip of paper, "That blackguard is here again," and pushed it across to Harry. He read it and looked across at me.

"Are you all right?" he asked.

"Yes," I said. No other word passed.

We had taken tickets for the Madison Square Roof Garden, and we left the Café Martin about nine o'clock and arrived at the theatre a little after. The show was a rather trifling kind of production called "Mlle. Champagne," and we stayed just long enough to be bored. Harry and I sat together, and we talked of nothing in particular save the merits of the play, and when I had expressed a wish to leave the theatre he was at one with me and we rose and went.

I have been asked so often to describe my feelings on that particular night, and my impression of the tragedy that followed after our leaving the theatre, and I reply invariably that I have no particular remembrance of what I was speaking of or what I was talking about. I know it was something very commonplace. If you were sitting in a restaurant with a man, and suddenly saw him rise, raise his hand and shoot dead at a man at the next table, without any warning, without any preliminary exhibition of temper, you would sit aghast and dumbfounded, and exactly what occurred and of what you were thinking before the outrage would be a matter rather for your imagination than for your memory.

We did not go immediately, but when we did McCaleb and I went ahead and Harry and Mr. Beale followed. We had almost reached the elevator, and I was talking to Mr. McCaleb and turned round to get some confirmation of what I had said from Harry, when I found to my surprise he was not there. I walked round to where he had gone. The next thing I remember was seeing Stanford White at a table about thirty feet away. For a moment I could not see Harry . . . then I saw.

He was standing about five feet from Mr. White directly in front of him. He had his hand outstretched perfectly still. Then I heard three shots. I could not have prevented it even if I had been at his side. I could only raise my hand to my lips. "My God!" I said, "He's shot him!"

Harry turned and walked towards me.

I said, "Harry, what have you done?" What have you done?"

He leaned over and kissed me.

"It's all right," he said smilingly. "I have probably saved your life."

Mr. McCaleb at my side was white and shaking. "My God!" he said, "You're crazy!"

I saw a man come up and grasp Harry, then they led me away to the elevator. I drove straight to the house of a friend, and that night, while the police were searching for me, I sat thinking, thinking, reconstructing the scene again in my mind, trying to grasp its meaning, trying to realize where it all led. Here was the end of a tragic period.

Here was the secret public property. Here were all the intimate things of life in the million mouths of New York.

The pressure of Harry's finger upon the trigger had done more than send the swift bullet upon its terrible way. It had released the curtain, which hid us all from the gaze of the world. All these eyes that stared, all these fingers that pointed, startled me. I have a dim recollection of being haunted by an army of reporters. I see again the flaming headlines that told the world of Harry's mad act.

I had no time to think of White, of that great brain acting no more for good or evil. Terror is a violent form of egotism — and I was for the time being terrified by all that I heard and saw.

Rumor needed to work double shifts anyway.

Remember where I stood, what support was afforded me in that hour of trial. The attitude of the Thaws, though in an isolated instance kindly, was of the I-told-you- so order.

What more could one expect? Harry had married a chorus girl, had married one who had never been accepted into the fold—he had committed murder. There was little to choose between the crimes.

I saw Harry in gaol. He was cheerful and buoyant. He had no doubt as to the righteousness of his act or as to its wisdom. He never then or at any subsequent time expressed the slightest regret for his act.

The Thaws, to give them all credit, did not reproach him. They strained every nerve to secure the best advice, which it was possible to secure. They were nice to me because, as I think, they realized instantly how much depended upon my testimony.

Mrs. Thaw and I went frequently to the Tombs to see Harry, and it was on one such drive that a little incident occurred which will show something of the working of the Thaw mind.

I went so often to the gaol that I became a familiar figure not only to the officials but to the police who controlled the traffic of the street. They would hold up my car at a busy corner and stroll up to the side.

"How is Harry?" they would ask, and we would chat for a while in the big friendly spirit that is characteristic of the New York policeman.

I looked forward to these chats. They were very comforting, for I felt in some subtle manner that I was not only discharging a pleasant duty but I was getting on friendly terms with the enemy.

One day, when Mrs. Thaw and I drove down together, there was the usual congestion of traffic, and as usual the policeman at the crossing stepped up with a smile.

We chatted for a little while, though I could see out of the corner of my eye Mrs. Thaw sitting with frigid face and stiff back in the corner of the automobile.

When we moved on she turned to me with a shocked face.

"Evelyn," she said reproachfully, "How can you speak with these people? Don't you realize the social position you hold?"

I was very angry for I had no illusion as to the social status of the Thaws.

"Mrs. Thaw," I said, "You have got to realize that the social position your son now holds is associated with the Tombs Prison. He is on trial for his life, and anything you can do or that I can do to sway public opinion in his favor has to be done. With reporters watching our every movement and on the hunt for 'copy,' what kind of a story do you imagine it would make, if I turned up my nose at men whose social position is, at the moment, infinitely superior to Harry's?"

Mrs. Thaw was silenced but not convinced.

# CHAPTER VII
# THE TRIAL

Consultations with lawyers, with the police, with reporters, occupy the full space of my time.

I am to tell the story of Stanford White.

It gives me a nasty taste to think of it; it filled me with horror when I first understood I had to do it.

It is an unthinkable thing that I must stand up in open court and tell . . .

But there is no way out — nothing less will serve, and Harry's life is in the balance. After all, what does it matter?

I tell myself this a hundred times a day.

Other women have gone into Court and told stories, without so much as turning a hair, which were infinitely more discreditable to them, but I feel my youth and the future looms up very black.

Nobody doubted that I would hesitate to lay bare my soul. The Thaws took it for granted that I should be pleased to have this opportunity. It shows Harry in the light of a saint, and that is enough.

I hinted that the evidence might discover him to be something else — but was "s-s-sh-ed" out of a hearing by his relatives.

For my own part, I am determined to tell all that will help him, yet there is a very patent alternative. It is a question whether any human being should suffer as I must suffer, on the witness stand, however momentous the issue. I have read in books of heroic prisoners who have risked death rather than the honor of their wives should be questioned. Harry's heroism is not of that variety. The newspapers would know nothing about it, and Harry is not the kind to be satisfied with posthumous honors.

Harry is sometimes ridiculously pleased with himself. He seems to look forward to my appearance in the box as the lecturer anticipates the utterances of a friendly chairman. I am to introduce Harry as Sir Galahad.

"Wait till my little wife gets on the stand," he told the reporters proudly, "and you'll hear a story such as you have never heard before."

I do not share Harry's enthusiasm.

The Thaws will put the biggest lunacy experts that money can buy on the stand. They can prove Harry was a madman, but they will prove it nicely. There will be no suggestion that he can be unpleasantly mad, or that his madness can take beastly shapes.

Somebody I spoke to on the subject smiled.

"Do you know Jerome, the District Attorney?" he asked.

I knew him, and nodded slightly.

"Jerome loves lunacy experts," said my friend. "He just enjoys them. You are going to see and hear things when Jerome rises to cross-examine."

He mentioned a few instances of Jerome's skill.

"Most lunacy experts like to be on vacation when a case comes into Court in which they and Jerome are engaged. I should not back the lunacy 'bugs' if I were you."

Ridiculous as it may seem, with the tremendous consequences hanging over their relative, the Thaws wish "to avoid scandal!"

A newspaper says that Harry is taking a great deal of interest in his trial. I can well believe it. Here is the trial at hand. The plans of the defense are not yet complete, though attorneys have been retained. Some one says that even the prosecution has not quite made up their minds as to the course to be pursued, but those who know Jerome say that he will confine the issue to one point: Did or did not Harry Thaw kill Stanford White on the evening of June 25th.

If this in the only question to be decided, the case will not last very long.

The trial has begun. It has already lasted three dreary days. Here am I with a crowd of other Thaws and a greater crowd of people who are Thaws or anti-Thaws in sentiment, and a judge on the bench who is neither one thing nor the other, and would be glad to be both.

The jury were empanelled after a succession of wrangles, and, true to the forecast, Jerome has delivered the shortest of addresses to them. Witnesses came and went. It was an easy matter to prove the offence—not so easy a matter to justify it. This man saw the shooting, this man arrested him, this doctor described the injuries in language that was mercifully unintelligible . . . and the defense came with a rush.

Mr. Gleason, Harry's attorney, put a mental expert on the stand. He put him on the stand to prove that Harry was nicely mad, and he proved it good.

Then arose Mr. Jerome, and for the space of a second they blinked at one another, the alienist with forced ease, and the square-jawed lawyer, all brain and ice-cold logic. It was an interesting day—it was also a little formidable.

For there would come a moment when I should occupy that chair and face this remorseless man.

There had been talk of hereditary influence in insanity.

"Are you acquainted, as you sit here," asked Jerome, "with the forms of insanity which the law of this State defines as excuses for crime?"

"Not entirely," replied the doctor.

"Then your opinion is hypothetical," said Jerome cheerfully. "The question you have answered was given as a scientific and medical man, and you had in your mind the various forms of mental aberration which scientific men meet together to discuss?"

"Yes," said the doctor eagerly, "and from my own application of medical knowledge on the subject."

His view was ordered struck out.

"What is your opinion, based on the form of insanity laid down in the law of the State?" asked Jerome.

"The act—the murder—was that of an insane man," said the other decidedly.

"Are you a psychologist?" asked Jerome.

"No."

"Have you studied the subject?"

"Not extensively."

"As a matter of fact," asked the District Attorney ironically, "do you know what psychology is?"

"Yes," snorted the indignant doctor.

"You say a delusion is the result of a pathological condition?"

"Yes."

"Then Thaw's delusions must come from a pathological condition?"

"Yes."

"Then Thaw's delusions must come from a pathological condition?"

"Yes, coupled with a functional condition."

"It is possible for a function to be abnormal unless there is disease?"

"Yes; a dilated artery, for example."

Jerome's eyebrows rose.

"But a dilated artery has nothing to do with the case of Thaw?"

"No."

The doctor was rapidly getting rattled.

Jerome put a question regarding the Romberg test used to diagnose brain trouble, and our expert, after some hesitation, had to confess that he did not know exactly what it was.

Jerome was truly at home with this type of witness. He led him through a mass of questions dealing with the pathology of insanity that at times seemed thoroughly to baffle the unfortunate man, who hesitated time and again.

Jerome seemed to have every medical authority at his fingertips, and the care with which he had prepared himself to meet the plea of insanity was manifest in every question.

The District Attorney's shrewdness was shown when the Court returned from an adjournment for lunch, in the course of which I had had a long talk with Harry, who seemed a little depressed and irritated by the attempt which was being made to prove him mad.

"With whom have you talked during the recess?" was the first question Jerome put, and the doctor was a little staggered.

"With Mr. Gleason," he replied.

"Did you talk about the case?"

The witness hesitated. "Yes. One gentleman told me the Romberg test was a test for locomotor ataxia."

Jerome jerked his head on one side and asked with an air of innocence —

"Doctor, does the cardiac nerve connect directly with the cerebellum?"

The doctor hesitated.

"Well," asked the attorney genially, "maybe you can tell us if the pneumogastric nerve joins the spinal column in the lumbar circle or the dorsal region?"

Again the hesitation.

"The dorsal region," replied the doctor.

Jerome smiled genially.

"Where is the dorsal region?" he asked, and the witness moved uncomfortably.

"I have not read much on that," he admitted.

"Oh, well, never mind," said Jerome airily.

"Tell me if it is not a fact that the pneumogastric and cardiac nerves are one and the same thing?"

A blow for the poor doctor. "They may be," he confessed.

Jerome dropped all pretence at geniality.

"Don't you, as a specialist in nerve diseases and an expert, know which is which?" he thundered.

The doctor was wisely silent. He was silent, too, whilst Mr. Jerome rained question after question on him.

"What books on nervous diseases have you ever read?"

The doctor mentioned two and seemed relieved to be able to do so.

"Do you recollect a single thing either of these authors said?"

"Not in their language."

"When did you last read them?"

"Just before coming here."

"Why did you do that?"

"I merely glanced at them"

Jerome looked at him with a little gleam in his eyes that I came to know so well.

"Dr. Wiley," he said slowly, "if you recall anything you ever read in any book please state it to the jury."

An invitation that was not accepted.

The torment went on anew.

"Are you a homoeopathist?"

"No."

"Well," said Jerome wearily, "What are you?"

"I am a nervous practitioner," said our expert in a loud voice.

"Is it not a fact," asked Jerome, "that all the functions of the human body are controlled by the pneumogastric nerve acting trough the spinal marrow or medulla oblongata?"

Nobody heard the reply. A roar of laughter swept through the court that the bailiff had some trouble to suppress.

"Do you know of the Argyll Robertson test of light?" asked the suave Jerome.

"Yes," defiantly.

"Where did you ever hear of it?"

"I do not recall."

"Did you ever hear of such a thing before I asked the question?"

The doctor hesitated, but Jerome went on thumping the table before him.

"Where, in any book in God's whole world did you every hear anything about the Argyll Robertson test?"

The doctor did not reply.

"Is Argyll Robertson one man or two?"

"I think two," ventured the witness.

Again Jerome's cynical grin.

"As a matter of fact he is only one man," he said.

"Did you ever examine this defendant regarding his sanity?"

"No."

"Have you seen him often?"

"Yes, in Pittsburgh."

"Can you determine whether a man is insane by looking at him?"

"No, I must have a conversation with him."

"Have you ever conversed with Thaw?"

"No."

"Do you think," asked Jerome, "it right that you should come here to give it as your opinion that a man is insane when you have not submitted him to examination and have not even conversed with him?"

"I gave my opinion on a hypothetical question, not on examination," said the doctor.

Altogether a bad day for us. I do not think Jerome likes medical experts.

Jerome has told the reporters that "he will do nothing to Mrs. Evelyn Thaw when he gets her on the stand," and those who find pleasure in the mental anguish of their fellows prepare for a threat.

Yet I am not afraid of Jerome. Before the trial I was in a store in New York, and the man, pointing to a number of picture postal cards, said —

"Do you know that man, Mrs. Thaw?"

I saw the portrait of a square-jawed man his finger indicated.

"That is Jerome," he said.

I took the card home and studied it. I never fear these square-jawed men. The theory of the physiognomies that strength is found in the bulldog chin is the greatest of all the fakes. Nor did the news that he intended tearing me limb from limb and exhibit the interesting remains triumphantly inspire me with anything but amusement.

I do not despise the terrors of cross-examination.

Small wonder that people wish to avoid the witness chair as a priest the devil! The fear of cross-examination is increased tenfold by the fear of publicity, especially if the case be of any interest to the newspapers. I remember a verse from a musical comedy that hits the nail on the head—

> Every one's record is a secret more or less,
> a trifle chequered, although people never
> guess.
>
> Cut up your capers—
> But don't get them in the papers—
> For you're done for, if you once get in the
> Press.

It matters not who or what you are, there is always a chance that you may be dragged into some case. As May Mack says, "These be days of exposure." All you have to do is to read the daily papers, and in their columns you will find one "prominent" person after another "shown up," divorces, sued by some star-eyed siren, and the like.

Now I want to say something for which I shall most likely be severely criticized, but I think it is necessary. It is right and proper that you should have a great respect for the law, the Court and its impressive ceremonies, even the Court officers and clerks, but don't take them too seriously. Most witnesses are overawed by the solemnity of the Court and the proceedings, seeming to lose their wits and apse into a state of mental numbness pitiful to behold. However, as I said before, don't take them too seriously. After all, the judge himself is only a man, and probably not half as learned and solemn as he looks, and for all you know may have got his job through some political juggling.   As for the lawyers, they may be leading double lives themselves.

In an important case the judge and the lawyers are themselves worried for fear of making some blunder.  The eye of the Press is watching them as well as you.

You are politely presented with a subpoena.  Immediately you begin to howl for a lawyer.  Mr. Lawyer soothes you, but not too much.  That would be spoiling business, from his point of view, for the less you are soothed the more you have need of counsel.  If you are to be a witness you naturally want to know all about it—what will be asked of you—will you be cross-examined?  A lawyer usually evades such questions, saying, "Don't think about that now, and wait till the time comes." The most they can tell you is what Mr. Delmas told me.  Said he, "My dear child, I cannot tell you—no one call tell you—what questions Mr. Jerome will ask you.  He himself does not know as yet.  You must do the best you can, and I will protect you to the best of my ability.  That is all."

A pleasant prospect—nicht wahr?

Here then is my advice to any witness—

The first and most important thing is to keep cool, for a rattled witness is hopeless.   Lawyers well know this and therefore do their utmost to rattle you.  For instance, a sneering, insulting, brutal method of questioning will upset many witnesses, especially women, while a suave, clever, polite questioner can lead an unsuspecting, truthful witness into hopeless contradictions, and he or she will never realize they had been trapped until it is all over.

Dress quietly.  If you are a woman wear something dark and plain and simple; avoid swathing yourself in all black, as that gives the impression you are dressed for the occasion.  Also avoid a hat with a plume on it, for the papers always describe such hats, no matter how small—"she wore a huge picture hat covered in plumes."

82

Understand each question thoroughly before answering.

Never be in a hurry.

Also don't hesitate obviously.

Be extremely careful about volunteering information.

Give your lawyer time to object—that's mostly what he's there for.

Be perfectly willing to answer all proper questions.

A favorite lawyer's trick is to ask a witness two or more well-thought-out questions at the same time—answers of which are contradictory—the one answer demanded being "Yes" or "No."

For instance, immediately on putting such a question to me Mr. Jerome would shout: "Answer Yes or No." Well, I knew I didn't have to do anything of the sort, and right then and there I'd start an argument and demand that the questions be separated and then asked one at a time. Of course, the Court would order the District Attorney to do so, and would instruct me not to answer any questions I did not understand, and the learned District Attorney would get rather rattled himself and pretty sore, which was perfectly sweet of him from my point of view.

Be careful about admitting signatures without examining them carefully. Abe Hummel is still somewhere about.

Never lose your temper unless the situation really calls for a display of righteous indignation—even then, know what you are saying.

Be truthful. Even a well-made lie is easily broken down under proper and persistent cross-examination. A witness who deliberately and knowingly commits perjury is not only doing a wrong but is a fool.

I offer these suggestions because they are the outcome of my own experience.

I was to learn them from a new phase of the game as it was shown to me on the day of my cross-examination.

It was not to proceed without confusion.

There were wrangles as to the admissibility of evidence; wrangles as to Harry's sanity. Harry looked wonderfully cheerful, I thought, and nodded a smile to me.

First Delmas took me in hand and produced the story of the Pie Girl. I speak of the Pie Girl because there are all sorts of stories concerning her and because in some mysterious fashion it has passed into the legend of the case that she was me. I reproduce the story from the official records—

"Did you and Thaw discuss the fate of the Pie Girl?"

"Yes. That was in Paris, in 1903. He asked me what other girls I knew of who had suffered at the hands of White. I told him I had heard of the Pie Girl, whose name was known to both of us. A girl at the theatre had told me about it, and that night when White came to my dressing rooms, I asked him about it.

"White wanted to know where I had heard the story, and I told him a girl had told me. Then he told me all about it.

There was a stage dinner, White said, and this girl was put in a big pie with a lot of birds. She was very young—about fifteen—I think he said.

He told me the girl had a beautiful figure, and wore only a gauze dress. He helped to put her in the pie, and to arrange it, and he said that was the best 'stunt' he had ever seen at a dinner, when the girl jumped out of the pie and the birds flew all about the room.

At a dinner party at the St. Regis Hotel in 1904, when Thaw, another man, and I were present, a guest told Thaw the story of the Pie Girl, giving all the details, and remarking that White had some trouble in keeping it out of the newspapers. He had told the man who was telling the story that he had gone on his knees to the editor of a newspaper, imploring him not to publish the story, and that finally, through the influence of a friend, it had been suppressed."

"What newspaper was it?"

"The *New York American*."

"What did Thaw say?"

"He said he must investigate it."

"When did he next talk about it?"

"In Pittsburgh, after we were married. He said he had investigated the story, and had found out that it was true; that afterwards the girl had got married, but her husband had heard the story of her relations with White and had cast her off, and she had died in great poverty and disgrace."

# CHAPTER VIII
## IN THE BOX AGAIN

The moment had come, the moment which I dreaded and welcomed.

"Evelyn Nesbit Thaw," shouted an official, and I made my way slowly to the stand.

I did not underrate the ordeal that awaited me. I knew that on my evidence would depend Harry's fate, and I knew, too, that a merciless prosecutor, the most skillful man in his profession, would leave no stone unturned to discredit me. I went into Court that morning with all the sensations of one already condemned, yet with the firm resolve to tell everything I knew; to bare my soul to the gaze of the multitude, so that in doing so I might help my husband. It would mean torture to me — it would mean perhaps everlasting effacement; it would certainly make me notorious. I was no better and no worse than any other normal being confronted with the prospect of having her most intimate secrets dragged into publicity.

I had a natural shrinking from such an experience, and my panic was accentuated by the knowledge of how much depended upon my statement.

Harry's eyes met mine as I took my place on the stand, and he smiled encouragingly. I knew that a friendly counsel would draw the first part of the evidence from me, but the story would be one that no woman could tell without an effort. In many ways I found this first day the worst of all, worse indeed than the cross-examination that was to follow. Nothing obscured my view of Harry, who sat about forty feet away in the center of the court.

I was now used to the Court, to the crowd, to the staid judge on the Bench. I was familiar with all the formula of the law; to the rows of busy reporters, to the spectators, to the acoustics of the building. But as I sat in the witness chair it was all the difference between watching the sea from the beach and viewing the beach from the sea.

Very slowly the counsel unfolded the story from my lips. First the actual shooting and all that happened on that dreadful night, then the meeting with White and all that followed.

Then he led me through the events that preceded the marriage.

As the case proceeded I found confidence. I could listen with patience to the wrangles that came up between Mr. Delmas, Harry's counsel, and Mr. Jerome.

It dawned on me that this trial was a game — a game played according to set rules. There were certain things you must not do, certain things that could be done, and others about which the rules were obscure. And because the rules were obscure they must make new ones as they went, appealing to the judge for confirmation.

When I realized this I began to take an interest I had not felt before.

Mr. Delmas spoke of a letter Harry had sent. Mr. Jerome objected to the letter being produced. Why?

They talked, and talked, and talked; first one and then the other, and then the judge. It must be a wonderful letter to produce so much discussion. Mr. Jerome would not have it. Mr. Delmas insisted. Why, I thought, so much bother about one old letter unless it proved something very vital? It was part of the game; it was like arguing whether you should play solitaire with the right hand or the left. The letter was forthcoming eventually, and was about nothing except mother sailing for New York.

Then Mr. Delmas wanted to produce another letter and Mr. Jerome was very insistent upon its not being produced because there was no date upon it. Another was very important because the judge said it must not be produced, and he said this very impressively.

I was a spectator for most of the time, and I grew impatient. I wanted Mr. Delmas to come back to me and get to important things. He turned to me at last and I was disappointed. He wanted to know things which I though everybody knew by now.

It was all very trivial and unimportant and banal, but it was part of the game.

"When you returned to Europe in 1903 did you come at the same time as Thaw, or alone?"

"I came before he did."

"Before you left Europe did you have any conversation with Thaw about your being met on your arrival?"

"Yes. Thaw said he would get Longfellow (his attorney) to meet me and see me through the Customs House."

"Did you bring letters for Longfellow from Thaw?"

"Yes."

"When did you first see Thaw after your return?"

"I think a little over a month afterwards.

"Where?"

"At the Hotel Navarre, where we were stopping."

"Did you see him alone?"

"No; I would not see him alone."

"Had he been made aware of this?"

"Yes, he had been made aware of it, and when he came to see me there was another man present."

I must stop here to whisper the name of the man. It seems it was a dreadful thing to be associated in this case.

"This second man was a member of the Bar and a person of standing in the community, was he not?"

"Yes."

The examination for the day ended tamely soon after this. It had been a terrible day for me, but worse for Harry. As I repeated the story of Stanford White, Harry's anguish was terrible to see. From time to time he strained forward in his chair and gripped the table convulsively, and when I had finished recounting the progress of my friendship with White he broke down and sobbed. The papers said that the whole of the Court was similarly affected, but so great was the strain on me that I did not notice this.

In order to introduce the contents of some letters put in I was recalled at the end of the day. One of them, which Mr. Delmas read, I heard for the first time.

"Evelyn has left me six or seven letters and telegrams from the blackguard. If they wish to begin a row I am ready for it, but I prefer to reach New York so as to go to Philadelphia, Pittsburgh, and Port Huron in time for the wedding on November 19th. I would return to New York in time to meet Lady Yarmouth, who lands on the 24th. The more row the better. Maybe we shall be married after Lady Yarmouth arrives; maybe after the row. Her mother don't count."

After referring to some unnamed married woman as a trickster and a schemer, and cautioning Mr. Longfellow that the marriage must be kept secret, Harry continued —

(He had written this when the absurd talk of a kidnapping charge was in progress.)

"If a suit for kidnapping is begun it must not be mentioned, but we will need two staffs of reporters... Miss N. would give all she possessed if I could have sent her to school instead of him. She should never have remained on the stage so long, and if they had listened to me she would not have. It resulted in her name being falsely connected with two others beside that blackguard. Poor girl, she was poisoned when she was fifteen and a half years old. Remember, if I die my property will all go to my wife, but in the event of her death it must not go to her relatives. Poor girl, if I die she may not live to be twenty-one."

90

## Friday, February 8th

The excitement created continues to grow. The crowds in the streets adjoining the courthouse are larger than ever, and the corridors of the building itself were completely congested. In the street under the "Bridge of Sighs," which connects the courthouse with the Tombs Prison, is an eager crowd, hoping to catch, through one of the windows, a glimpse of Harry as he passed.

When he is brought in this morning, instead of walking briskly to his place as usual, he seemed to move in a hesitating way, looking about to right and left in the crowded courtroom. His pallid face broke into a faint smile as he recognized his brother Edward, the only member of his family then present.

It is difficult to describe the peculiar sensations produced by extreme nervousness. A tight drawn feeling in the throat, sharp pain in the wrists, a weakness along the spinal column, and in the knees. If any one spoke to me suddenly my heart began palpitating in a frightful manner. The assembled lawyers, doctors, and witnesses were tactfully silent.

Suddenly we heard the court clerk's voice ring out, "Evelyn Nesbit Thaw."

"Well," I mused as I entered the courtroom and passed behind the jury box, "the worst they can do is to kill me—so here goes."

There was intense silence except for the excited rustling of paper from the Press tables. When I reach the witness stand, a court attendant handed me a Bible; this I held while being sworn, which is a rather impressive business. The clerk looked at me in a manner evidently meant to be earnest and said, "You do solemnly swear."

To which I mechanically bowed my head, stepped up to the witness chair, and sat down. It was anything but pleasant to face this courtroom. Immediately in front of me sat Jerome, his assistant, Garvan, Dr. Austin Flint, Dr. Carlos McDonald, Dr.

Mabon, and some friends, evidently, of Jerome. To left the jury, and to right Justice FitzGerald; beyond the railing at the end of a table sat Harry Thaw, flanked on either side by a great deal too much counsel — six in number. Delphin M. Delmas, his partner, Henry Clay McPike, Daniel O'Reilly, Clifford W. Hartridge, A. Russell Peabody, and John W. Gleason, a handwriting expert, David Carvallo, numerous sleuths hovered about, to say nothing of the specialist, Dr. Smith Ely Jellife, Dr. Britten, Dr. Evans, etc., etc, all charging small fortunes merely to lend their presence to the scene. Next came the long tables of reporters, some of them special writers, Irvin S. Cobb, Charles Somerville. In the extreme right corner sat the "sob squad," the majority of these, especially the females, looking like a lot of special lunatics. The friends of Jerome who sat inside the railing close to me, with arms folded, legs crossed, and wise expressions, eyeing me with the expression which the Romans of old devoted to the early Christians before the lions were loosed into the arena.

Delmas took me again.

There were letters to be read and identified — mainly letters from Harry. They were sad letters, despondent letters. One was signed "From one about to die," which was so like Harry in a certain mood that I almost smiled. There were letters in which he boasted of his power in Pittsburgh — of what he could do there if he wanted. He could control it politically — this was like Harry, too, only in another mood. He was troubled about the stories White had circulated.

"Alone I cannot settle down. Besides, I have no one worth doing it for. Twice I had to leave the table so that they could not see. But in some ways I am a bear at times; in other ways I am more cheerful. I am not responsible now. You must know that every story is a fake, except one. I saw all those letters and they are all sham but I don't care a little brass. You know me better than anyone. If you don't trust me, and know that I am true and unselfish compared with most men, then there is no hope for me. I am changed now, but not in truth, faithfulness and courage. Promise me one thing. Don't drink champagne. I am too poor, and must live at home. I can't pay for you ring now. Of course, if you are in need, I can get loads of money, but it would make trouble. I must stay here or get a cheap ticket East. Of course, don't say anything about this."

There was, of course, no truth in the story of his poverty, but it was Harry's way to go the limit either in joy or sorrow. Delmas wanted to know about my association with White after I returned from Europe, and I told him all that I have set forth in this book.

I note that even friendly lawyers have a habit of going backward and forward, as the mood takes them. Mr. Delmas would return from America with startling abruptness and reappear in London with breathless speed.

"Did Mr. Thaw, while you were in London take you to see his sister, the Countess of Yarmouth?"

"Yes."

"Where?"

"At her home in Berkeley Square."

"How were you received?"

"Very kindly."

The day's sitting dragged through. There were constant interruptions in the giving of my evidence. Jerome must protest and Delmas offer solemn explanations, and at the end of the day I found myself a thousand miles, so it seemed, from the end of business.

When the Court rose, the door through which I had to pass was blocked with people, and I had to wait. I was very tired and dispirited.

**February 20th**

Jerome's line of examination is now plainly indicated. It is clear that he does not intend to spare my feelings, and presses

93

his questions sharply as to the details of the dresses I wore when posing for artists in the Philadelphia and New York studios, persisting in certain queries and insisting on definite answers, despite the protests of Mr. Delmas. He credits me with a memory I do not possess.

"Where did you mother live after coming to New York?"

"In West Thirty-sixth Street, between Fifth and Sixth Avenues."

"What was your first theatrical appointment?"

"In the *Florodora* Company."

"You contributed to the family support?"

"Yes."

I am a terrible girl by inference. My "No" sound very feeble in comparison with the detailed and impressive questions Jerome puts.

Now I am keeping questionable society.

"Did you become acquainted with Mr. M—?"

"Yes."

Now I am a cunning destroyer of evidence.

"Were those letters among the packages of letters which you burned after taking them from a storage warehouse in this city?"

Delmas objected to what he described as "this amazing question," declaring that there was no justification for it, and Justice Fitzgerald sustained the objection, though it made little difference to me what form the question took.

"Did not you take out letters from a warehouse?"

"No."

"Did you visit a warehouse?"

"No."

"When were you first ambitious to become a great actress?"

"Before I went to Philadelphia."

"Then, when you came to New York, had you still this ambition?"

"Yes."

"What did your mother think about your going on the stage?"

"Mother said I ought not to go out without her. She said the 'show' was all right, but she ought to go along with me."

Mr. Jerome wanted to prove my own slackness from the moral standpoint. He produced some photographs that had been taken of me. They were disappointingly proper.

"Are these fair types of all the pictures taken that day? Are there none suggestive on any more impropriety than these?" he asked aggrieved.

"There were some taken with a low neck." I said encouragingly.

"Was there any further exposure?" he persisted.

"They were very low neck," I replied.

Mr. Jerome was getting exasperated. There was one point upon which he hoped to shake me from my calm into a condition of agitation. That was the question of money that from time to time Mr. White paid whenever I was out of an engagement. Again and again he returned to his subject—an unsavory one, as all questions are into which money enters.

I have explained that these sums came to me because Mr. White acted in a duel capacity towards me. He had taken upon himself the task of furnishing me with a career. In that capacity I knew him first and best. That I could remember every detail was not to be expected by anybody but an attorney who desired to discredit me.

"Were you informed in January that a sum of money had been deposited for your benefit?"

"I am not sure of the date."

"What was the amount?"

"I don't remember."

"Was it a large or small sum?"

"I don't remember."

"Did it make any impression on your mind?"

Asked Mr. Jerome in exasperation.

"No," I replied.

"When did you begin to doubt that proposition?"

"When I went abroad in 1903."

"When Thaw proposed to you," sneered Jerome, "and you rejected him, did you believe yourself to be better than others because of what happened to you?"

I could afford a smile. That was not the way to rattle me.

# CHAPTER IX
## THE *DEAD RAT*

**February 21st**

After my cross-examination the different members of the Thaw family made a great fuss over me in the witness room and at the hotel. I was "brave little Evelyn" and "dear little Evelyn" and "most courageous girl," and "wonderful, bless her heart." Had the lawyers told them I made a bad witness they would all have shown unmistakable signs of desiring to shake me, so I am not pleased with their praise. Anyhow, after their enthusiasm dies down their feeling will undergo a violent reaction.

I feel sorry that the interest of the case has shifted from Harry to me. I feel more and more confident in myself. That Harry's life is at stake is an issue seemingly forgotten in this duel between myself and the Public Prosecutor, practiced in tearing the hidden secrets of lives from witnesses in the chair.

His pitiless rain of questions, however, does not impair the consistency or truthfulness of my story. Here is a Press comment that pleased me.

"From one point of view, the cross-examination's effect tended rather to strengthen the defense's argument as to the cumulative effect upon Thaw's mind. There was never any faltering, and as her courage rose, more than one answer having every semblance of candor and innocence parried Mr. Jerome's questions by producing an *impasse.*"

Jerome did not like that.

The District Attorney took me to Paris this morning. He is a great traveler.

"Did you continue to believe that all women were unchaste, as White told you, until you talked with Thaw in Paris in 1903?"

"Yes, sir," I said meekly.

"Do you know a place called the *Dead Rat*?"

"Yes." (Poor *Dead Rat* how terrible you look in English!)

"Where is the *Dead Rat*?"

"It is somewhere in Paris."

"Have you ever been there?"

"Yes."

"What sort of place is it?"

That Mr. Jerome should ask this question! "It is a café," I replied.

"Is it a reputable café?"

"I don't know."

My "don't know" and "can't remembers" are worrying Jerome.

"Did it seem reputable to you?" he demanded ominously.

"I don't know," I said; "people were sitting about eating."

It seemed a respectable thing to do.

"Was there somebody dancing?"

"I think so."

"Was it two o'clock in the morning?"

"Possibly."

There seems to be something particularly sinister about two o'clock in the morning.

"Did you see the cakewalk being danced?"

"No. I think it was a Russian dance."

As a matter of fact I round afterwards that it was cakewalk, which in the ante-ragtime days was considered very smart indeed.

Jerome would not leave the *Dead Rat*. I suppose it sounded very wicked, though it was a most innocuous establishment.

"How many times were you at the *Dead Rat?*" he demanded with relish, and was not pleased when I told him only once.

Who was with me? Again I must whisper names. The "Dead Rat's" association was almost as bad as association with myself.

Be it understood that if I speak lightly of Mr. Jerome, or if I speak a little bitterly, I have now no longer any sense of resentment.

I realize that he was doing his duty to the people, that he was and is a man of great integrity and power, and that he was actuated by no sense of personal malice toward myself.

That he probed me cruelly was not his own desire. He had a case to make out, and he was prepared to go to extremes to make out that case.

But there came a moment in his cross-examination when he broke through all my reserves, and for the first time—and the last—he brought me to tears.

The line of interrogation that led to this climax was as follows—

"Did you refuse Thaw solely because of the occurrences in which White was concerned?"

"It was because I had been found out."

"Who told you that you had been caught?"

"Friends of White."

"So it was not because of the occurrence, but because you had been found out?"

"It was both together," I replied. "I had an instinct about it when Mr. Thaw proposed. It was the first proposal I had ever had, and it struck me very seriously. It all came together."

"Had you felt the heinousness of the wrong that had been done you?"

"I did not know anything about it at the time."

"It outraged every instinct in you didn't it?"

"It did, and that is why I quarreled with White."

"You were very bitter against White when you told Thaw, were you not?"

"Not then."

"When you felt that you were giving up Thaw's love did not you fell bitter against White?"

"Not intensely; not until Mr. Thaw made me realize it."

It was true that I did not feel enmity against White at that time."

Now we are back once more in New York.

Before your talk with Thaw did you believe that meretricious relations between men and women were immoral and wrong?"

"Oh, yes," I answered. It is strange how quickly one gets to such a condition of mind that such matters can be calmly discussed.

"Did you think them indelicate and vulgar?" he persisted.

"That is all."

"That it was bad taste?"

"Yes."

"But didn't you think it was wrong?"

"I didn't fully realize it," I answered, and I spoke the truth.

Jerome pressed me as to all that had happened in New York. There was no evading him. He asked me questions that made me hot and cold. All the experience of the previous days was of no avail; there came a question. . . . I broke down.

Jerome came back to the *Dead Rat*. It wields an irresistible fascination over him. Now I understand why he asked me about the cakewalk. In my exuberance I had written a letter to a friend.

"Your suggestion that the Tenderloin has immigrated has panned out. Everywhere we go we find shady nooks. Shubert and a lot of others are here. We were dining at the Café de Paris the other evening when a whole bunch came in. We joined parties, and went out to such harmless places as the *Dead rat*. There was one jolly man who puts on the blink wherever he goes. He is fifty years old but as spry as a chicken. We took him along for fun. We made things hum, and started home when the markets were getting busy. Harry bought some strawberries, and I spent the next day cooking them. Harry is getting a new automobile, and as soon as it is ready we are going to Schweitzer (cheese) land. Then when we return my voice is going to be cultivated. Be good, and whirl me another letter soon. Your letters are wonderful."

A letter, which I identified as being in Harry's handwriting, also referred to the *Dead Rat*, "where," it ran, "we met Miss Winchester, and got her to do the cakewalk at two a.m. It was a great hit. Rosenfield and Belmont were there."

There was another break in my evidence to allow a witness to take the stand, and I was recalled to face Jerome later in the afternoon.

We came to White again. White — White — always White! It made me go hard and bitter to hear the name of this man whose dead hand was laid upon me.

"White had a strong personality." I said, and Jerome listened, his eyes fixed on mine. Outside that one awful thing White was a very grand man. He was very good to me and very kind. When I told Mr. Thaw this he said it only made White all the more dangerous. Before the Twenty-fourth Street incident, White never made love to me. He always treated me with the greatest respect and kindness. Everyone liked him, and nobody would believe these things until they really found them out, and then they said they were sorry."

## Monday, February 26th

They recalled me again today. Three days rest and quiet has made a wonderful difference. I have seen Harry in the Tombs, and he has been cheerful. Somehow one cannot feel sorry for Harry; he will not allow that liberty! He is in his heroic mood, which is irritating. The dreadful seriousness of the position in which he stands does not seem to impress him so much as the sudden fame that has come to him. He is forever making statements to the reporters and gives me the uncomfortable feeling that he is enjoying the experience. Jerome comes after me today, but I was quite at ease. I knew that he would try to prove that I am something worse than the dust—that is his business. A good lawyer never sees two sides to any question; there is only one side—the side he is on.

He dragged up every incident that might be magnified to my discredit, and hopped from one aspect of the case to the other with agility worthy of a better cause. Had I quarreled with my mother in Allegheny before I lived in Philadelphia—had I run away from home—he might have asked me whether I had committed murder in my youth, and received no greater satisfaction from my replies. Had White given me money? When? How? He had given me presents for my vacations and had helped me along when work was slack. Had I gone to supper ever with this man or that?

(Names whispered with a great show of secrecy and the speculations of the spectators aroused to fever pitch.)

Yes, I have supped in the same party, but not with them. It would not have affected the issue greatly if I had so supped.

Did they take me home? Had I a chaperon with me? Were these suppers after the theatre?

I had an absurd desire to make extravagant and inconsequent replies. That supper should come after the theatre was not remarkable. Had it come before the theatre it would have been something freakish.

Then back again to White and to his vacation allowances and to the little sums he gave me from time to time.

It was impossible to point out the fact that he had established himself in a dual capacity. That he was a self-appointed guardian, a man of sufficient authority and domination to pack me off to school at his pleasure.

Then on to Harry.

Where did I first meet him? When?

"At Rector's Restaurant, at a dinner given by Mr. Thaw. It was after a matinee, and the dinner lasted about an hour. I was accompanied by another girl," I added hopefully, for this question of chaperonage seemed a very important one.

"Was Thaw rational during that dinner?"

I nodded.

"He was not excited?"

"No."

Jerome wanted to prove that Harry's desire to meet me was of itself an eccentric act. A poor compliment to me.

"When he came to pay for the dinner," said Jerome slowly and expressively, "did he not require help in counting the change? Did he not require anyone to tell him the denomination of bills?"

"No."

"He was perfectly rational?" persisted Jerome.

"He was perfectly rational," I repeated.

"Did Thaw, during the first weeks of your acquaintance, give you any presents?"

Harry had sent me violets, and mentioned this. A straw for Jerome, but he was no despiser of straws and seized it.

"Was there anything about his manner in sending the violets to attract undue attention?" he asked.

I smiled. "Nothing, except that they were very beautiful."

Again I had the sense of playing a game—a game with big forfeits in which the acute mind would always score. It was stupid to be irritated by the apparent futility of the questions—it was part of the game too.

"Did he ever send any money with the flowers?"

I replied "yes."

There was an occasion when Harry had sent me fifty dollars, and at the suggestion of the stage manager I had returned it.

"Was this before or after he called? You cannot remember? Did it make no impression on your mind?"

"Yes, that is why I remember it."

A note for witnesses: It is not the insulting character of questions, or the embarrassing character; it is the very triviality of the questions that causes a witness to lose patience. And beware of such a question as this sandwiched between trivialities.

"You were not in the habit of receiving money from men?"

For a moment I nearly lost patience, then in a flash I realized I lost a point if I lost my temper and replied. "No."

"How many times had you seen Thaw before he sent you money?"

I had recovered now. The emphasis he put upon "sent you money" left me cold.

"I couldn't remember," I said.

"Didn't it strike you as strange?" he insisted.

I knew it was always done at the theatre, for I had seen it going on all the time, and I said so.

"Did it impress you as to the nature of acquaintance you had reached?"

"What do you mean?" I corrected though I knew well enough what he meant. The fact that Thaw returned the money would come later. For the moment was necessary that he should impress the jury.

"Did you know him well?"

"No."

"Did your mother make you send the money back?"

"No"

"Who did send it back?"

"I did."

Jerome knew that I had sent it back, but that was part of the game.

"How much was it?"

"Fifty dollars." And I added, "When I next saw Mr. Thaw I asked him not to do such a thing again, and he apologized." I was learning the rule quickly: a witness might add things to her reply and discredit a question if she is quick enough.

"Did Thaw seem self-possessed at the time?"

"Yes."

Then followed a succession of questions designed to show me in the light of a frivolous character.

"Did you go to the costume supper at the Hoffman?"

"Yes."

"When?"

"Late in the summer of 1902."

"Was Thaw present on that occasion?"

"Yes."

"Were you in a costume?"

"Yes.  It was a hired one."

"Were there other women present?"

"Yes."

"How many men were there?"

"I don't remember."

"When did the party break up?"

"About 2 or 2:30 in the morning."

A supper party without men and without women that broke up earlier than two o'clock would have been a cheerless festival.

"When did you next see Thaw?"

"Not for a long time.  He went abroad."

"How many times did you see him up to June, 1902?" Asked Jerome.

Here is a type of question that no witness can answer definitely and is brought out because of this reason.

"I can't say," I replied.  "He called several times."

"Ten or fifteen times?" asked Jerome with the air of one who knew.

"I don't think it was as many as fifteen."

As I have said, Jerome was not satisfied to pursue any consequent line of examination.  From the question of my own decorum to Harry's sanity was a step.

"Up to February, 1902, had you noticed anything irrational about Thaw, either in his appearance, in his actions, or in his manner?"

"No," I replied.  To say that there had been moments when my doubts were aroused would have involved me in a maze of semi-contradictory explanations.  Besides which, up to that

106

time, he had not proposed marriage to me, nor were his attentions to me at that time more marked than those of other men, and my casual recollections of a man who did not greatly interest me would have been unfair to recall.

He questioned me about other men. "Other men" were Jerome's trump cards. To blacken my inference, to suggest rather than to state that I had liked this man or that I helped him out of every bad patch in which he found himself. Did I sup with this man? Had I met that man? —With dramatic swiftness Jerome turned and indicated one who stood up in the Court—had my name been associated with this gentleman?—so the questions ran on and on and on.

Then back again to Harry.

"Did I understand that Thaw was paying honorable court to me?

"What do you mean by courtship?" I asked, and Jerome, who is no sentimentalist, floundered, to my amusement. It was one of the few smiles I had in the proceedings. Since I was no clairvoyant I could not know whether Harry had matrimonial intentions during the first period of our acquaintance.

Did I travel under an assumed name in Europe?

"No."

What was the effect of my story on Thaw? — Jerome had heard, but I must repeat it.

Did Harry carry arms? Didn't he pull out a pistol while he was with me in a Paris restaurant?

To both questions I had to answer no. It seemed to me that Jerome was making his case as he went along, that he was searching haphazard and for information that he did not possess. He would pursue every side issue with this object in view. Where had I gone on my return from Europe? To what hotels? Did I love Harry? Who paid the bills at the hotel? I replied that I did.

"With whose money?"

"My own."

"Where did you get it?"

"Mr. Thaw gave it to me."

"Was it cash or deposited to your credit?"

"It was cash."

"Did you ever see Thaw take cocaine?"

"No."

"Did Thaw ever tell you that your mother believed he had kidnapped you?"

"No."

"Was there not some talk of a suit against Mr. Thaw for kidnapping you?"

"Not that I ever heard of."

"Were you depressed after your return to America in 1903?"

"No."

The questions were beginning to tire the Court; there was a stirring and a shuffling of feet. Jerome came back at me with a more brutally direct question.

"Did you ever receive money from White after you became reconciled with Thaw?"

"Never in any way, shape, or manner," I replied.

Again I felt my indignation rising and had need of a tight rein upon myself.

Then back came Jerome to the European trip.

"When you went to Europe, what names did you travel under?"

He had asked the question before in another way. He asked it now as blandly as though he had never before mentioned the subject.

"Mr. Thaw went as Harry K. Thaw, and I as Evelyn Nesbit," I replied.

From Europe to America again the tireless prosecution went. This time it was to Abe Hummel and the famous affidavit.

"When you went to Abe Hummel's office you had a talk with him?"

"Yes."

"Didn't you tell him the details of your trip to Europe?"

"Yes."

"Did you tell Hummel that you had found a hypodermic syringe among Thaw's effects? Didn't you tell Hummel that Thaw had threatened to kill you?"

"I did not."

Harry was an interested listener. From time to time he smiled at me, and only once did he interrupt the proceedings. That was when at Jerome's request a man rose in the body of the Court for me to identify. I failed to do this, and then Harry leant over to the reporters and whispered.

"That man is a liar — do you get the point? — A liar!"

# CHAPTER X
## MORE REFLECTIONS ON THE TRAIL

Jerome has given his views on me and I still survive. It was a wonderful speech, probably the finest forensic effort ever made in New York's law courts. Seldom has an address to a jury been so full of relentless logic or cruel, biting sarcasm. He aimed most of his shafts of ridicule at the "angel child" and "her Sir Galahad millionaire lover from Pittsburgh." He argued that if Stanford White had been a common Eastside art dealer, if Thaw had no millions behind him, if both had been quarrelling over a cheap Bowery chorus girl, all the talk about brainstorm would have been laughed out of Court. The tragedy was nothing more nor less than a common, vulgar murder, prompted by a fit of sordid jealousy. He spoke at an extraordinary pace, but every word bit.

The concourse of eager spectators this morning was enormous. For fully two hours before the opening of the Court, which had been fixed for 11:30, the public began to arrive, and occupied every position of vantage. The corridors leading to the courtrooms were impassable, and the Court attendants had to use the side doors to admit the personal friends of those concerned in the case and others supplied with the necessary passports. When the doors opened at eleven o'clock there was a tremendous crush, most of the seats in the Court being already occupied by those who had been admitted privately. The space in front of the bench reserved for counsel, the members of the Thaw family and their friends were also crowded. Altogether the scene when Jerome rose to address the jury for the prosecution was one of tense expectancy. Scores of disappointed men and women who had tried to rush the guards at the doors and force an entrance had to be fairly dragged away from the corridors.

Mr. Jerome began his address by saying that an appeal had been made to the sympathy and the passions of the jury, which constituted a broad departure from the duty of counsel. There could be but one of four verdicts—murder in the first degree, murder in the second degree, manslaughter, or not guilty because of insanity.

"You must," he proceeded, "reach your verdict by a purely and plainly intellectual process, as you would dispose of a problem in geometry, an equation in algebra, or a sum in arithmetic. You are the sole judges of this issue, and you are to judge by the facts. You must not decide upon the opinion of counsel on either side, or upon that of the Court, except in regard to the law as laid down by the Crown. You cannot shake your personal responsibility by evading it. Both sides may play the matter of sympathy in this trial.

Whether you believe the story told by this girl, whether you believe in the sublime 'renunciation' she made in at first refusing Thaw's offer of marriage for another whim, your sympathies are bound to assert themselves in one form or another. But when you retire to consider your verdict you must lay aside all that, and guide yourself solely by intellectual processes."

Then he came to me, and I braced myself for his candor.

His voice, which was under admirable control, rose in a great wave of emotion and gradually sank again to a pitch of intense passion.

"How strange it is, my friends," exclaimed the District Attorney, "that this 'angel-child'—this girl of the chorus—should believe what she says Stanford White told her about all women being bad, and some simply so unfortunate as to be found out.

Does what she says afterward appeal to your common sense? Does she shrink from this man? Does she abhor him? No," he thundered, "She meets him again and again.

This dragon preying upon female virtue wrote this 'angel-child' letter after letter, scores of them. We have shown them to be in the possession of the defense. Some were identified, but

112

was a single one put in evidence or read? No; there is nothing to show that these letters contained anything bad. Now contrast this with the modern St. George who led the 'angel-child' back to the paths of virtue, and In November, 1903, writing her a letter in which he discussed perversion."

I had been honest about White—I had spoken honestly about him. I expected little generosity from the District Attorney, and I was not agreeably disappointed.

"Now, gentlemen, let us see what this girl says about the horrible demon who had ruined her. She says, 'Outside this one awful thing I admired Stanford White. He had a most extraordinary personality.' What an extraordinary panegyric coming from those lips! Stanford White's lips are sealed by death and the rules of evidence. But what are we to believe against this man to whom such a tribute is paid by this girl? Her own words have ruined the theory that Stanford White was a brute. He sees this child blow into his circle. You have looked on this girl in Court and can well draw a picture of her at the time she applied for an engagement in the *Florodora* chorus, and was told by the manager that he was not conducting a kindergarten or baby farm. It was natural that White should have tried to help this girl. He helped her to an extent. When she was out of her work he gave her money. It was natural that he should give her little gifts of wearing apparel that tended to her comfort. There was nothing in his conduct inconsistent with the theory that the relations between the two were pure. You have not a scintilla of evidence that heir relations were not pure outside this girl's story.

We know what this sort of life is—the life of the stage. We pass along the city's great white way (as Broadway, when illuminated at night, is sometime called), and we see something of that life. Why, think of this girl beginning her stage career, with men paying her attentions, Thaw following with his presents of 'American Beauty' roses and money.

We see the whole situation centers about this girl, which it was she who in the long run brought about this crime. So I will

113

give you a deeper insight into the life and thoughts of this 'angel-child.'"

Mr. Jerome then proceeded to read extracts from the diary I had kept at school, explaining that he had received it, not from her mother, but from the police.

"I have been rebuked," he continued, "because it has been said that I sneered. It seems to me that there is certainly ground for a sneer when the word 'virtuous' is placed in quotation marks by this girl."

He found fault with the dress I had worn during the trial. What it had to do with the great issues involved I could not say.

At which allusion I smiled.

I went home that night and made an entry in my diary.

The school diary was an awful blow. When Jerome first handed it to me and I saw it, I almost perished, for the mere fact that it was a silly school diary, written over three years before, was enough to unnerve an ox. What had I written? There was nothing to do but to sit still and read it through. The most damaging material Jerome could find in it he had blue-penciled. Occasionally I glanced at Jerome and there would be a decided twinkle in his eye. This diary was written in 1903 when I was a pupil at the De Mille School in Pompton, New Jersey. There I had gone, straight from Broadway, carrying with me some choice George Ade[10] expressions and considerable slang. The choicest morsel of the lot was "pie-faced mutt," which Jerome had carefully blue-penciled. I heaved copious sighs of relief, for, after all, that was not so bad.

All my past is out now, even a foolish school diary!

Mr. Delmas: "Mrs. Thaw, will you permit me, right here? You have mentioned the name of a certain lady whom I do not

---

[10] George Ade, 1866–1944, An American humorist and dramatist. His newspaper sketches and books attracted attention for their racy and slangy idiom and for the humor and shrewdness with which they pictured people of Midwestern America.

know, and I would request of you, if the request meets with the approval of the District Attorney, that is giving your narrative you omit, unless he shall insist on it, the name of any other persons connected with any of these events except that of Stanford White."

Mr. Jerome: "I think that is a very proper request. I concur thoroughly with you in that. I think it is most eminently proper."

Mr. Delmas: "I had intended making that request before."

Mr. Delmas, it will be observed, was clever enough to get ahead of Jerome in making this tactful request, thereby bringing upon himself the undying gratitude of certain "prominent persons: who were in an agony of fear lest their names be dragged into the affair."

At the close of each Court session Judge FitzGerald would admonish the long-suffering jury thus: "Gentlemen of the jury, allow me to again repeat the instructions given you, that you must not form or express any opinion regarding the guilt or innocence of the accused until the matter is finally given to you at the close of the case, and you must not discuss the subject among yourselves."

There was a lengthy argument over the introduction of the will of Harry Thaw. It was in the possession of John B. Gleason from the time it was received in Pittsburgh, and he prided himself that no one had seen it until it was produced in Court. He called a subscribing witness, Frances E. Pierce, to testify to the genuineness of the document, without ever showing it to her until she was on the stand, when he produced nothing to refresh her memory or even informed her as to what she was called for, and the woman could not even identify her own signature and did not know what the document was. The will was admitted in evidence upon the testimony of John B. Gleason, who identified the documents.

(Found this in a newspaper and made a copy of it.)

"The irony of the situation must somehow have struck even the figures of Justice and the Three Fates which look down from the wall of the Court when the Public Prosecutor today called for his principal witness Abe Hummel, the lawyer, whom only a year ago he had convicted of conspiracy and placed under an indictment for perjury. His testimony was now expected to shatter the credibility of Mrs. Evelyn Thaw's story, and the interest of the observers rose to the culminating point.

Hummel was to testify that the charges made by Mrs. Thaw against Stanford White were false; and to support a copy, partly a photograph and partly a carbon duplicate, of the affidavit signed by Mrs. Evelyn Thaw in White's tower rooms after her return from Europe, when she quitted Thaw for the time being, and renewed her friendship for White, was to be presented to the jury. Mrs. Thaw had sworn that she was led to make this strange affidavit without knowing that Hummel had dictated it to his stenographer, despite her protest that her signature to it was obtained by the trickery of White, and that when later she returned to Hummel's office and demanded it along with certain letters, the letters were returned, but the paper, which she was told was an affidavit, was burned. She saw it put in the fire. The prosecution avers that Hummel had taken the precaution to photograph the document, and the defense objects that such secondary evidence is inadmissible."

The rest of the morning was a pleasanter sail fro me, though I had to read that infernal diary of mine. It took some time to read, and if an expression of amusement flitted across my face as I recalled certain mental phases of that stage of my existence in an environment totally dissimilar from that in which I found myself before and after, it is not be wondered at. Jerome wanted certain phrases submitted to the jury as inconsistent with what might be expected from a pure-minded and ingenuous girl. I think the jury was disappointed. They expected something of the abnormality of a Marie

Bashkirtseff.[11]   They were, as a matter of fact, the natural reflections of an intellect in the cub stage of development.

Hummel is a very little man, and the big stenographer who came with him blotted him from view.  Jerome did not relish his task, but he went at it.

"Did you have a conversation with Miss Nesbit in your offices?"

Delmas objected, but the question was admitted and the witness answered "Yes."

"Did you dictate to a stenographer while she was present?"

Mr. Delmas again objected, saying the purpose of the District Attorney was to contradict my evidence, and he could not properly interrupt the cross-examination of that witness for such a purpose.

Hummel said that he did dictate the affidavit in the presence of Miss. Nesbit.   He was also allowed to say that the stenographer gave him the paper on the following day, but an attempt to identify what purported to be a carbon copy of it was ruled out on the grounds that it was an attempt to controvert collateral facts brought out in cross-examination.

Then I came back to the chair, and that infernal school diary of mine was put in evidence.

Mr. Jerome handed me some papers, and asked me to identify them as a diary I had kept in 1902.

The diary was written while I was at school at Pompton, New Jersey, to which White had sent me.

It was such a diary as youth dictates and exuberance executes, and I confess that I had qualms, for who shall bind the impertinent tongue of sixteen or give it restraint?   One extract spoke of a certain youth as a "pie-faced mutt"—the vulgarity of it!

---

[11] Marie Bashkirtseff  1858-1884 was a Ukrainian born Russian diarist, painter and sculptor.

Another said, "My room here is neither large nor small. There is white virtuous bed. I took a map of it, and the last thing I remember was that I wondered how far I am from Rector's Restaurant. Rector's is really not a proper place for an innocent young person, but I always had a weakness for it.

When one comes to think it over, it is good to have lived. A girl who has always been good and has never had any scandal about her is fortunate in more ways than one. On the other hand, none of them will ever be anything. By 'anything' I mean just that they will, perhaps, be good wives and good mothers, but, whether it is ambition or foolishness, I want to be a good actress first. . . If I stay here long I will be just like the rest, very susceptible, and I shall soon be. . . " (Here, Mr. Jerome explained solemnly there appeared three exclamation points and a pen sketch of a nun.)

The eternal question was set up against me.

"Did you ever see anything in Thaw's conduct that was irrational?"

"Yes," I said, and I detailed several instances.

I had seen Harry excited at the very sight of White.

"I don't know what you would call it," I said, "but I would call it a fit." For Harry had cried and sobbed.

"Did you ever see a man in a fit?" Thundered the sarcastic District Attorney.

I thought awhile.

"I have seen cats," I replied in all innocence. There was a roar of laughter, though I had not intended being funny. Even the grim Jerome smiled.

"Well, did Thaw act like that?" I told him "Yes."

"At that time did you think that he was of unsound mind?"

"Yes, on the subject of White."

"So early as 1903 you thought him crazy on that subject?"

I nodded.

"Yes. Stories were being circulated about us by White, and I found out that White was having things about us put in the newspapers."

"Were others besides White concerned in this persecution?"

There had been, and I whispered a name.

"Did Thaw complain that White had prevented him from being elected a member of the Knickerbocker Club?"

"It was some club, I don't remember which."

With that they let me out of the witness stand, though by this time I had become quite at home. But to be dismissed by the District Attorney was the equivalent of the dismissal by a cat of a mouse. His long paw would lick out and haul back the victim at a second's notice. So would the more gentle paw of Mr. Delmas, and after a while he had me back again to identify a number of checks and receipts, which showed mother had received various amounts from the stipend deposited by White on my behalf.

Delmas then handed me several photographs of myself, and asked by whom I was posed for those pictures. I replied that I was posed for most of them by the photographer in Twenty-second Street, to whom White took me.

Among the pictures brought into Court were those contained in a large album that White had arranged and presented to me. In this collection Harry displayed keen interest, placing it on the table in from of him and poring over its pages.

Mr. White and his money were fertile subjects for discussion. It was the one point that the prosecution could make against me, the one point on which Delmas, to my embarrassment, desired elucidation.

I had not spent a penny of the letter of credit given me by White on my visit to Europe, but my mother saw something in a shop window at Boulogne and asked me to buy it for her out of the credit, and she did so.

"Did Thaw hear of this?"

"Yes, when we were in Paris he wanted to know where mamma got the 'waist' she was wearing and I told him. He replied 'You didn't spend the letter of credit money, did you?' and raised a fuss, saying I should not spend it. He took the letter of credit from me, so that mamma should not spend any more of it. She got the rest of it, however, after returning to New York."

Once I had run away from Harry. It was so slight a story that I have not told it in my diaries, but nothing is too petty for examination in court, and the full story came out.

One day I had met a girl in the street, and she told me Harry had been paying attention to her. I went back to the Grand Hotel, packed a few things, took my maid, and got a carriage. As we were starting I had met Harry, who asked me where I was going, but I would not tell him. I drove straight to the York Hotel. As I was going into the restaurant I met a young man I knew. He went into the restaurant and sat down with me and afterwards we went to the theatre together. After the theatre we walked back to the hotel, and I asked the young man, who was living there, whether he could get a room for me without registering. He did so, and I said "goodnight" to him. That is all there was to it. Next day I met a girlfriend in the street, and told her what the other girl had said to me, but she said the other girl was a bad woman, and that I should not believe her. Then I thought what she had told me wasn't true, and I went back to the Grand Hotel.

# CHAPTER XI
## "OBJECTION DAY"

**February 12th**

I remember this day as the "Objection Day." Everybody objected to everybody. The game was getting very complicated around about here, and a little wearisome to the amateur.

You saw that there were mysteries to which you were not initiated, and that legal proceedings could be a business that was monstrously protracted.

A question that to my inexperienced eyes was perfectly innocuous would be asked. Up would rise Mr. Jerome (or Mr. Delmas) with horror and dismay written largely upon face —

"I object," he would snap, and all the players of the game would explain to one another why the objection was made, why it shouldn't be made, who made it thirty years ago, the circumstances under which it was made, why another judge ten years later had overruled the objection, what everybody had said about it then, why the ruling of twenty years before should be sustained, and so on, *ad nauseam*.

We started the day with a discussion of an objection regarding Harry's will. Mr. Jerome withdrew the objection. Then I came back.

Mr. Delmas asked me what the note contained that I had passed to Harry at the Café Martin on the night of the tragedy.

I replied, "The blackguard was here a minute ago, but went out again."

"Did you ever hear Mr. Thaw refer to threats against his life by White?"

Jerome objected. A plea of self-defense, on the defendant's own statement, was inadmissible.

121

Mr. Delmas replied to the objection that these threats had been made, and it was competent to prove that Thaw had armed himself after hearing of these threats.

Question not allowed, but Delmas persistent.

If he could show that Harry's statements were the result of insane delusions he would have the right to put them in evidence. Question not allowed, but Delmas made a note of the objection.

The next question was whether Harry had told me that malefactors, who had been set upon him by White with designs upon his life, followed him about.

Jerome objected. Objection sustained — Mr. Delmas makes another note.

"Did you ever see a pistol in Mr. Thaw's possession?"

"Yes."

"When was the first time?"

"I cannot say exactly," I said, thinking hard, "but it was some time after Christmas, 1903."

"Do you know whether the defendant ever carried a pistol anywhere except when he was in New York?"

"Never, except when in New York."

Mr. Jerome objected to the piling up of cumulative evidence without an essential fact being shown.

Delmas replied that he was trying to prove Harry's mental condition by evidence as to his looks, his acts, and his declarations. Harry was, he said, temporarily insane, and he was trying to show it by a series of acts, before and after the occurrence of the shooting.

Objection sustained, and the exasperated Mr. Delmas demanded whether he was to understand from the ruling that all conversations between the witness and her husband were excluded.

The judge was cautious. He thought certain matters had been gone as far into as they deserved.

But Mr. Delmas resume his inquiries on the same point. Mr. Jerome again objected — objection sustained.

"What effect did the presence of White have upon Mr. Thaw?"

Jerome was up again, "I object," he said, almost automatically, and the question was disallowed.

"Upon your return from Europe in 1904, by the North German Lloyd steamer, was Mr. Thaw present on the steamer?"

"Yes, sir."

"Do you remember Mr. Thaw, while you were on the steamer, telling you about what happened to a certain young girl at the hands of White?"

"Yes."

"I object," said Mr. Jerome, wearily.

Objection sustained, and the industrious Mr. Delmas makes a note.

"When you were in Paris did you tell Mr. Thaw about a young woman known between you as 'the Pie Girl'?"

"I object," said Mr. Jerome, and I was similarly debarred from answering another question regarding what Thaw told me when I finally accepted his proposal of marriage. Nor was I allowed to tell what Thaw had said to me concerning certain statements he had made to the Society for Prevention of Vice.

Somewhat discouraged, Mr. Delmas withdrew me.

Harry was very cheerful at the afternoon sitting. While some letters were being read he engaged in an animated conversation with Mr. Peabody, one of his counsel. He was in exceptionally good spirits, smiling from time to time, nodding with emphasis, and apparently finding the break in the tedious proceedings something of a relief.

Here I would remark upon the letters that have been introduced into Court. I never realized people wrote so many letters. It seemed that the world had been writing them with the object of producing them in Court. To my untutored mind they were not letters that proved anything one way or the other. They were inconsequent; they dealt with matters as far removed from the subject in hand as San Francisco is from Yokohama. If John Brown lost his dog on Twenty-second Street on the day I met Stanford White his letter was produced with much solemnity. If Trixie Smith went to dinner at the Rat Mort on the day I was married her letter was produced, read, objected to, and passed *con gusto*.

These are, of course, purely fanciful illustrations, and I adduce them only to show the confusion in my mind that these documents excited. They bewildered me and they bored me. It was unfortunate for the prosecution that no letters that were really relevant to the case had been written. In this matter we had all been singularly remiss. I had not written to anybody to say that the man I cared most for in the world was at the moment a lunatic, that Harry had written nothing of his secret sentiments about Stanford White. Well might Jerome moan with the prophet:

> "Oh that mine enemy had written a book."

**February 19th 1907**

Harry, as I have said before, was quixotic. He was knight-errant whose actions were mainly dictated by selfishness. I say that in the nicest way. He was not disinterested either in his likes or in his dislikes. His campaign against White, to which reference was made at the trial, is a mystery to me in many ways. He hated White for a good reason; he waged war against him for other reasons. He had cause for his animosity, and one of the causes was fear—the variety of fear that comes to a man who is set upon injuring another and conjures up vision of reprisals.

Throughout the piece he seems to have been quixotically anxious to keep my name away from the affair—he was satisfied to cite other instances of White's wrongdoing to justify his actions. Yet in the crisis he committed the act which of all others would place me in the forefront of the scandal. He was in the unhappy position of sacrificing himself to save others and sacrificing me to save him. I say, without bitterness, but with the conviction of one whose curiosity has worked out a peculiar situation, that Harry was one of those warped martyrs who deputize their cavalries.

To those who know all the circumstances and who pity him—as indeed every human heart must pity him for his very deficiencies—I would say that Harry's mania is of such a form that contentment with himself and approval of his own actions more than counterbalance the discomfort of confinement.

I say this the more readily because these is no aspect of the trial and the events which led up to the tragedy to which I have not given the most careful thought and study. There is no book intelligible to the lay reader that I have not read and understood. I have seen Harry Thaw in the big, cold light which science throws upon him. I have read many impassioned and impartial accounts of him and of myself written by people who are frankly prejudiced either for or against me, in the hope that I might extract from their frenzy one grain of common sense. I know Harry now better than I have ever known him, and I am satisfied with my own judgment. All this leads up to the introduction of Harry's will—an introduction which was strenuously opposed, but which was eventually made.

The will and its codicils made a curious document, and in it one read of Harry's obsessions.

The battle over the introduction of Thaw's will ended this afternoon when Mr. Delmas, as leading counsel for the defense, read the codicil which made special bequests to young women who, in express terms, were designated as having innocently suffered the same treatment as I. In his will Harry left funds for investigating the circumstances of his death, should that take place under suspicious circumstances (the fear of his being done to death for his philanthropy was always uppermost in his mind), and he gave bequests to his personal servants, which he placed under the charge of his sister, then the Countess of Yarmouth.

The reading of these documents came rather as a surprise. Mr. Jerome had Dr. Evans on the stand, vainly trying to get him to commit himself to a statement under what particular form of delusional insanity Thaw was laboring in making one of the codicils.

I never say Harry look so self-possessed as he was when the will was read in Court — though at this time he was having a bit of trouble with his legal advisers. His eyes were bright, his dress was neater, and he was cheerful in his attitude toward his counsel, seated on either side, and to the mental doctors, one or other of whom sat beside him. It made an incongruous situation, this calm, self-possessed young man, listening interestedly to Dr. Evans describing his symptoms of lunacy.

"He gave me his hand," said Dr. Evans, telling of a visit he had made to Harry in the Tombs prison, "and looked at me with a staring and twitching of the eyes and a nervousness such as we seldom see. In an agitated manner he asked me to sit down beside him on his cot. He looked at me for a long time, and then said, 'you've got different eyes from Dr. Hamilton. Your eyes look as if you were a sane man, his suggested insanity.'"

"I asked him how he was, explaining that I had been sent by his counsel. He said I was all right if I came from Mr. Hartridge, and in reply to the question how he felt, he exclaimed, 'Oh, I am all right.' These words were nervously uttered and piled together. Then he continued, 'There is a lawyer in conspiracy with Jerome so as to close this matter up

126

and railroad me off to an asylum. They wanted to have me declared insane. It's all rot; there's nothing in it. They don't want me to come to trial, where I may be vindicated.'"

Harry had told him he had not wanted to kill White, but had sought to bring him to trial, and would rather have humiliated him thus. I remembered the interview. It was one of the countless times Mrs. Thaw and myself had visited Harry, and we had arrived while the interview was in progress. Dr. Evans offered to withdraw, but Harry had told him to remain, and after kissing his mother and me introduced the physician to us, asking us to excuse him until he had finished his talk with the doctor.

"As a result of a subsequent visit did you draw any scientific deductions from Thaw's action?"

"Yes, he displayed a highly-explosive mental make-up, in that, without adequate cause, he dismissed his counsel and the physicians after we had agreed in advance that we were to come there for the purpose indicated. He displayed defective reason in putting aside the professional men, who, he had been assured, were there through no unfriendliness."

"Have you read the codicil to Thaw's will?" asked Jerome.

"I read part of it, and heard it all." replied Dr. Evans.

I have said that Jerome does not love the lunacy expert, but in Dr. Evans he had a man of attainments very superior to those of the men who had previously passed through his hands.

The crowded Court settled down to hear Jerome at his best.

"What was the class of insanity from which Harry was suffering when he drew up the will?"

"That would depend upon the classifier," said the doctor cautiously. "I would call it developmental insanity."

"Was it paranoia?"

"No."

127

"Were the delusions you observed on your first three visits to Thaw systematized or unsystematized?"

"In a measure they were systematized."

"Were they systematized or unsystematized?" snapped Jerome.

"They were not altogether unsystematized."

"Was there an apparent delusion in the will of the codicil regarding White?"

The doctor looked at the will.

"Wait," cried Mr. Jerome. "I object to your looking at those documents. You have seen them and given evidence in regard to them."

But the Court did not uphold the objection.

"I withdraw the question," said Mr. Jerome.

"Then we withdraw our papers," retorted Mr. Delmas.

"Without reading those papers," asked Jerome, "can you state whether or not there was apparent delusion regarding White?"

"I do not say there is, but there is a delusion both in the will and the codicil."

An answer that did not satisfy the learned District Attorney.

"Point out in the will," challenged Jerome, "Any unsystematized delusion."

Dr. Evans started to read extracts when he was stopped.

It was not Jerome's best day, for his objection was again overruled.

Then was read Harry's famous proviso—

"In case I die other than a natural death, or if any suspicion attached to my taking off, or if I should be made away with, I direct my executors immediately to set aside 50,000 dollars for the investigation of the circumstances, and the prosecution of the guilty persons."

"Is that an unsystematized delusion?"

"One statement does not make a system," retorted the witness quickly.

"Can you point to any other unsystematized delusion?"

"I am unable to say."

There was another wrangle, but Delmas was allowed to read the codicil.

It bequeathed the sum of 7,500 dollars to be used in obtaining legal redress from White or another person, whose name was not mentioned, in favor of four young women, whose names were also omitted, whom the codicil declared had been ruined by White "in a house in New York, furnished and used for orgies by White and other inhuman scoundrels."

The codicil went on to recite the circumstances of the alleged assaults in the case of each of the four young women in question. It also left Dr. Charles H. Parkhurst, Frederick W. Longfellow and Anthony Comstock 2,500 dollars each for the purpose of securing evidence of any other assaults committed by White and obtaining redress for the victims.

Mr. Delmas read the entire will, and there was no objection by the prosecution, but the counsel, who in reading substituted the word "blank", did not name the recipients of ordinary bequests. The will leaves me 50,000 dollars, and established a trust fund of 50,000 dollars for me, while the residue goes to a trust fund from which an income of 12,000 dollars a year is to be paid to me.

During the reading of the codicil Thaw sat with his head buried in his hands, but when the reading of the will began, looked up quickly.

No question was raised as to the sanity of Harry when the will was made—it is the codicil that raises the subject of his condition of mind.

# CHAPTER XII
## MYSELF vs. THE THAWS

**March 8th**

My relationship with the Thaw family remains placid. Whatever their views may be upon their attitude towards me my perception of their positions remains unchanged. I think they are inclined to take themselves very seriously, and it may be that they have decided among themselves that they will adopt this or that manner. To me there is very little difference, though I am conscious of the fact that some agreement has been made as to how I shall be treated in the future. Whatever their plans may be they are so dependent upon Harry's fate as to make no difference for the moment.

Mrs. Thaw, who came to the stand today, is too absorbed in the big things of life to take any definite step one way or the other, but it is a curious fact that, despite the gravity of the situation, these people have time to think out such petty matters as the attitude of a society which hitherto has not overburdened itself with any great responsibility in regard to the social standing of the Thaw family. Mrs. Thaw made a good witness. She put up a fine fight for her son's life. Every motherly instinct was aroused. She is a kindly matron, with brown eyes and a pleasant expression. She was dressed in widow's garb, with her black veil thrown back, disclosing a mass of silver-white hair. At all times she was perfectly self-possessed.

Harry, who now showed traces of his prolonged ordeal and confinement, sat with his face buried in his hands, following his mother's words.

I found myself intensely interested in the evidence. I felt like one to whom certain secrets hitherto hidden, but long suspected, were to be revealed. What the Thaws thought of me I knew — what they would say I anticipated.

The evidence was at first formal.

In the autumn and winter of 1903 she was living in Pittsburgh. Her son Harry came home on November 16th or 17th, a day or two before his brother Josiah's wedding.

"During the time your son Harry was at home did you notice anything unnatural in his conduct?"

"Certainly I did."

"Will you please describe what took place?"

"On the day that he first came to the door there was a look of absent-mindedness on his face—a despairing look. It struck me at the time."

"Did that impression of your son grow on you?"

"Yes; he seemed to have lost all interest in everything. His room was next to mine, and often in the night from his room I heard smothered sobs. Sometimes when I was awake late at night I would see a light under his door, and I often found him sitting up until three or four in the morning. When I asked him why he sat up so late he told me that he could not sleep, and that it was no use going to bed. I am not of a prying disposition, but I asked him to tell me what was the matter. He said it was impossible to tell his story."

"Did he at any time freely, or in answer to you questions, tell you that story?"

"He told me freely one night when I insisted on his doing so."

Harry had told her the story. His troubles were caused by something a wicked man had done in New York—probably the wickedest man in New York. That man had ruined his life, and he would never be happy again. That was all.

Harry had seemed absorbed to his mother, as if he were working out a great problem. He was extremely fond of music, and he would heave the table, and go into the parlor. She would hear loud music on the piano, which would gradually grow softer, and he would come back to the table as if nothing had happened. He did this most often when there was company at table and he was engaged in conversation.

"Poor Harry! No evidence of insanity here, as I can testify.

"A week before Thanksgiving Day I understood more. I did not know what the girl's name was, and did not ask it. I did not want to know it, but I did now that his condition had something to do with a young girl. He had told me about a wicked man in New York, but it was only later that I found out that this man had ruined a young girl.

After I had found out that his condition was due to something that had been done to a young girl, I asked him why he should allow his life to ruined on that account, and told him it was not his duty to look after the girl. I tried to influence him another direction, but he protested that his life had been ruined, and told me the girl had the most beautiful mind naturally of all girls he have ever met.

He told me this about Thanksgiving time, and it cause me look at matters in a new light. He said there was still a chance for her to be good, and so on. I can't recall all he said. On Thanksgiving Day Harry and I were alone. The rest of the family was away."

Poor Harry again! A more wretched way of spending Thanksgiving I cannot conceive.

I give her statement as she gave it. The opening paragraph more than any other shows Mrs. Thaw and the interests that once were mine.

"It was the first Thanksgiving in our large beautiful new church, and Harry and I went to church together. It was so crowded that we had to sit well back under the gallery. I was glad it was so later, for when the choir was singing Kipling's 'Recessional' to Beethoven's beautiful music I heard Harry sob, and looking round I saw his tears falling on the programme he held in his hand.

133

I put out my hand and touched him. He was trembling all over, but I succeeded in quieting him. As we drove home I asked him how he had come so to forget himself."

Harry weeping at the Recessional was to Mrs. Thaw an amazing thing. That he should so "forget himself" was evidence enough of a disturbed mind.

"When did you first learn who the young woman was?"

"I cannot recall precisely, but I think it was in the spring of 1904."

"Can you recall any conversation you had with your son at that time?"

Mr. Jerome objected on the ground that there was nothing in the evidence to show that the prisoner was insane at this period. I feel inclined at this moment to agree.

"Did he speak to you again about the young girl?"

"There had been a horrible scandal, or, at least, they had made it out to be a scandal. I remember expressing my disapproval of his coming home in the same ship with the girl, and he explained it all to me, and said he still was of a mind to marry her."

"You have said nothing before about his wanting to marry her?"

"I must have forgotten it. He told me in November 1903, that he wanted to marry her, but that he had been frustrated. In February 1905, I took Harry for a trip to the South. He then asked me to come to New York and meet the young woman, and In March I did so."

"Was the marriage then under discussion, and was it finally arranged with your approbation?"

"Yes. It was not necessary that I should give my consent, but I did."

Here came the record of a conversation that was interesting to me.

"After meeting the young woman we returned to the hotel. Harry asked me if I had any objection to his marrying her. I told him it was not necessary for me to give my consent, and he said he did not want to do anything against my wishes. I then said I was perfectly willing. I did afterward make one condition, not to prevent the marriage, but I told Harry that if he married the girl and they came to my home to live, her past life must be a closed book and must never be referred to—I mean her life in New York."

Mrs. Thaw continued to refer to me as "the girl" and the "young woman." I might be excused resentment at this latter description, but I felt none.

"We arranged that the young woman should come to Pittsburgh and that she should be provided with a chaperon. When Harry came home from the wedding he seemed to be laboring under great stress. I feared the wedding would be interfered with by the young woman's mother on account of the girl's minority."

Jerome tackled one point of view that was new to me.

"Was the defendant's income fixed at a stated sum in his father's will?" He asked.

"Yes."

Jerome asked Mrs. Thaw to state Harry's income subsequent to June 1903.

"I am unable to say exactly. It was certainly not what the newspapers have said."

"Was that income from his father's estate?"

"It was from his own estate, inherited from his father."

"When your son returned to Pittsburgh in the fall of 1903 he expressed a desire to marry Miss Nesbit?"

135

"He did."

"Did he ever express a fear that others would prevent her from accepting him?"

"He said she had told him that it would be a very unsuitable match. I said if she came to me her past would be a closed book."

That was all. Harry had been upset because he wanted to marry me. I was a "young woman" who had come into the Thaw family; the past was a "closed book."

A closed book never to be mentioned in Pittsburgh society, but to be reserved for a crowded court where every other man was a reporter.

**April 12th**

If there are any other people in the world than we Thaws and Nesbits, the newspapers do not tell about them. If there is any other happening beside this trial the newspapers conceal the fact. Every page I see is filled with accounts of the trial for today; we shall know one way or the other how the jury regards Harry and his set.

I went to the Court relieved. The protraction of the trial has been terrible. My own life has been reshaped with some violence—looking back upon the period that covered the killing of Stanford White and the trial it seems like a nightmare. So familiar were the sights and sounds of the Court that I could not realize that this almost daily attendance at Court had not been a life-long practice, and that I have not been familiar with the Tombs from my childhood up.

There was always a little group about the doors of the prison to greet me when I made my visit. Always a cheery voice to ask me "How is Harry?" when I came out. The people were lovely to me; their kindliness and their sympathy helped me more than I can explain to bear up in moments when my nerves were all a jangle.

But here was the last day of the trial! The judge had delivered himself of his address, the old familiar ground had been traversed, and I had listened without a pang, without wincing, to the recital of a story that a few months back had filled me with panic at the bare mention.

Those months had been an examination and a test for me. It mattered as little to me then as it does to me now what people might think of me in my dealings with the world; I never once had a sense of apprehension as to what judgment Mrs. A. or Mr. B might pass upon me—the test had been applied by Evelyn Thaw to Evelyn Thaw.

I have spoken of Harry's egotism, and now I give an exhibition of my own. The trial meant as much to me as Harry—more, in fact. It is better for one's self-respect to stand in the public gaze as a culprit than as a victim. In the one you may be brutal or vicious, but you are strong; in the other, however pathetic a figure you may strike, you are weak. Yet the figure I cut before the world concerned me not at all.

Somebody wrote tearfully of my wasted opportunities—this was in the course of the trial. How, under more favorable circumstances, I might have been a shining figure in humdrum society; but I have never wanted to be that. I never desired the four walls of shapeless domesticity to imprison me. My marriage was a mistake. It took the mass of my soul and handed it to puny and inartistic sculptors for their shaping. I was rock crystal in their hands, and their blunt little chisels could do no more than chip and scrape and scratch.

They could not fashion me according to their design, nor could they impress upon my unsympathetic surface the dim image of their God. Harry Thaw was nearer to me in sympathy than any other member of this family—he alone made the life in the Pittsburgh home endurable. Cut out, the morbid obsession which filled him and he was as good a husband as one might wish for, and I was a patient and faithful wife. I had been determined to make him happy, and had, I think, succeeded. In a normal healthy man the past would have been forgotten. For my part, I was willing to forget much of his former eccentricities, which were less than creditable.

Well, here was the end of endeavor. A jury had been locked up all night deciding the fate of a man who was less suitable to domesticity than I. Backward and forward the jury had tramped—from jury room to Court, from Court to jury room. This evidence must be read over to them and that evidence. The judge's charge—even the speech for the defense that Mr. Delmas had delivered.

"Certainly not," said the astonished judge at the latter request. . . . It was terrible, that waiting. We all felt it.

As for Harry, he sent statements to the newspapers, one of which was to the effect that he had bathed that morning—he added sarcastically that the newspapers were evidently interested in such items.

During the afternoon there was a constant gathering of people in the streets leading to the Court building, particularly near the Bridge of Sighs. A big force of police failed to keep the crowd moving on.

When Harry was called to the bar today he entered with a quick stride. His eyes were bright, and in his arms he carried half a dozen morning newspapers, which he had been reading. He was in better condition physically than any other person connected with the trial. The dejection he betrayed on leaving the Court last night had gone. Last night while waiting for the expected verdict he was the jolliest member of the party. He bowed graciously to his mother, to me, his sisters the Countess of Yarmouth and Mrs. Carnegie, and his brothers Edward and Josiah, and then, turning to his counsel, entered into a brisk conversation with them.

After the retirement of the jury I went to luncheon with one of the counsel for the defense, Mr. O'Reilly. While passing along the street I was almost swept off my feet by the rush of people eager to obtain a glimpse of me, and Mr. O'Reilly had to fight a way for me through the throng. When we returned the mob had attained even great dimension, and the police were obliged to open up a passageway, hundreds of people, many of whom were women, trying desperately to get near. Scores rushed into the courthouse building, besieged the elevator, and climbed the stairs in their anxiety to see me, and the police experienced great difficulty in clearing them out of the corridors even after I had passed in. Other members of the family on leaving the building were also more or less roughly handled owing to the excited curiosity of the crowd.

I do not understand even now on what point the jury split. It was enough that they disagreed, and that the worst end to the trial was avoided. Harry was bitterly disappointed.

"If there is justice in the State I shall be acquitted," he had said to the reporters, and the family shared this view.

I confessed I was relieved by the disagreement. Even then I had few illusions, and certainly none that murder was anything but murder, or that a jury who had before it the undisputed evidence of the killing of one man by another could come to any conclusion other than that the bare facts as stated and uncontested were true. Nobody ever questioned the fact that on a certain evening Harry had shot dead Stanford White. Whether he was insane at the moment was the only question for decision. To anticipate a verdict of "Not guilty" without the rider as to his insanity was unthinkable, yet Harry did expect that, and so did his people.

The jury disagreed.

That is all.

Hollow-eyed men, too tired almost to talk, came blinking into the Court, red-eyed, husky, and shaking. I think I knew they had disagreed. It was common knowledge that they were divided.

Oh, well. There must be another trial, possibly yet another. The story told all over again, perhaps with greater wealth of

139

detail. For myself I had ceased to be horror-stricken, I was not getting to the limits of boredom.

And yet behind all this was Harry's life. I told myself as much a hundred times. Harry, who was my husband; Harry, who in his inconsistent way had been quixotic and kindly. Whether I loved Harry or not then or before is of no great concern to anybody. If love is sacrifice, then be sure I loved him; but there are other instincts beside love that induce giving. There is that innate sense of justice with which I was born, a sense of loyalty that has ever been mine, a faith in the genuineness of his desire to serve me, however mad-headed might be the way he chose.

Nonetheless the formality of denying this innuendo or admitting the truth of that suggestion had ceased to hold novelty or excitement for me. I wanted a change; I would have welcomed the most strenuous tussle with the lawyers providing they would take a new line—promulgate new changes and introduce into the dreary atmosphere that was mine something electrical to startle me to interest.

Here was the case over and with no further advance toward a solution than had been made before the opening day of the trial.

Harry was terribly depressed. The disappointment left him dazed and bewildered. His counsel had not shared his optimism, and, while the alienists—that young army of lunacy experts—had taken a view that a verdict in which his murder was established would be returned; Harry had not shared their enthusiasms. For he was satisfied that his fellow countrymen would have give him a more triumphant exit.

A man had been so acquitted on the Pacific slope. He had killed a man and had received the pardon that a Californian jury accorded him amid demonstrations and public approval.

Harry's interest in the case had been largely responsible for the murder. The man who did this was lauded. In Harry's eyes he was little short of a hero, and I do not doubt in my own mind that the events that had led to and had followed the acquittal were as much responsible for the crime as any.

The "exaggerated ego" to which reference had been made in the course of the trial was a very important factor in all that Harry did. The world revolved round him.

"I am Harry Thaw of Pittsburgh!" was the dramatic announcement he had made to me on our meeting, and in these words he told me all that I know about him. His self-importance was phenomenal, and he was talkative on the subject of his own virtues.

# CHAPTER XIII
# VIEWS ON PEOPLE

If Harry Thaw were sane his character was the most complex that I have ever examined. Had he grafted to his eccentric habits of thought a creative faculty he would have been a genius. I have observed that men who have the eccentricities of genius and none of its quality are sure enough insane folk. Examine Harry Thaw's actions, and see how much they lacked consequence—

- He himself was tinged with perversion in his relationships with women.

- He is filled with horror at the crimes of Stanford White.

- To shield me, he agrees with his family that the past should be a closed book.

- To justify his hatred of White, he keeps the book open.

- To revenge himself on White and because he feared him, he kills him.

- He takes this final step not for the wrong that I have suffered, but because a similar shooting inspires him, which left the murderer a popular hero.

- To save himself he plays his trump card—my life as a child—in every terrible detail. He boasts to reporters, as one preparing them for a great treat that they will have a story from me such as has never been told.

It is not my wish to follow the wary progression of trials and commissions in lunacy that was to send Harry to an insane asylum; for me it was a most terrible ordeal. Somebody once asked me whether I spoke the truth throughout all those examinations. From any but the person who asked, that question would have been impertinence. I spoke the truth—

every word of it. If I willfully suppressed facts they were facts that would have told against Harry. He was not giving me the happiest time; he was moody and hateful sometimes, insistent upon my appreciation of the fact that he had done everything for me.

I was not sufficiently grateful for the sacrifice he had made — he, Harry Thaw of Pittsburgh. He had killed the man for my sake; he had faced death for me, and I was not grateful. God knows I tried to argue him to a normal condition of mind. I tried to point out to him what fetters these were upon my gratitude. I could have told him of the sacrifice I had made to save him from the consequence of his mad act, but I had little urge on my own behalf.

I have observed that men are very sympathetic to sick women; only they do not believe that we ever get sick. This is a peculiar fact that has application to me. Everybody thought that I had conducted myself splendidly during the trial. I was "brave little Evelyn" and wonderful girl. A reputation for courage is the hardest reputation to uphold on the battlefield. There had been times when I was near to breaking down. I was a sick woman mentally and physically, and nobody seemed to realize the strain I had undergone — nobody except a few of those good friends who had stood by me in my darkest hours and understood me well enough to know how bitter was the ordeal through which I was passing. People would have been sympathetic — I do not doubt — if they had known I needed sympathy, but sympathy must come spontaneously to be of any value, such expressions I received were not very impressive.

There were the other trials ahead. I was quite a lawyer now. I knew the rules of the game. I saw the ponderous machinery of it, the aged cogs and flywheels that were so immovable in appearance as to suggest that they had no functions, save to add to the illusion of complication.

That those trials came you know. Criminal trial, examinations in lunacy — an age of litigation so it seemed: a whole lifetime spent in the choking environment of the courts. I learned my way to the Tombs. It was as familiar a road as I have ever trod. I learned the routines of prison, the faces of the warders, the situation of the cells.

Gradually the center of gravity was being changed. The question as to whether Harry killed Stanford White or not was all beside the point. We never thought about that. We were engaged in the pursuit of a new quest, the elucidation of a greater problem. Was Harry a sane man? Was he a madman only on that night of terror? "A monument of convenience." One of the opposition counsels described our pleading; another spoke of our "supreme audacity" in urging the plea we did.

Wrangle on wrangle, showers of mud darkening the air, long and wearisome periods of dull verbiage, and a never-ceasing tramp from the body of the Court to the witness stand and back again—these are the impressions I retain of those months—or where they years? —Of inquiry that proceeded the issue of a dictum that Harry was mad all the time and must go to an insane asylum.

We had saved his life and we had done that which was right to do, but in doing what I did I incurred the resentment and eventually the hatred, of my husband. To save his life we must prove him mad; to prove him mad I must adopt an attitude that was tacitly hostile to him: I must tell stories of our association which lashes him to fury. I must give to the world stories that I have locked in my own bosom. No other evidence could be so convincing as mine. Actualities will always succeed against hypotheses, and my experience with Harry carried more conviction than much of the medical evidence.

Not only must I antagonize Harry but I must earn the scowling disapproval of the whole Thaw family and lay the foundation for a complete estrangement, for it must be remembered that the Thaws "have a certain position in society to uphold" and no new story of Harry's eccentricities could succeed with the appointed arbiters of his fate unless it also brought the name into contempt.

145

Here was my position, and the impartial observer standing outside of my life will judge whether I did my duty and in what trying circumstances I so performed it. To be silent or to lie jeopardized his life, to tell the truth would save it.

It was folly to juggle with such big issues. Neither any other nor I could convince hardheaded legal folk that a man could be sane all his life and a lunatic for the space of three minutes. We have hoped for and had hanged on a verdict of "Not Guilty." We have persuaded ourselves that sentiment would rise superior to reasoning, that "the unwritten law" would carry my husband to liberty—and we had failed. We had to make the best of a bad job.

When the trial began I had taken off my gloves and handled the truth, however unsavory it was, without hesitation and without fear. This was no time to resume the gloves and mince with vital facts.

I saw Harry almost daily save for the time when considerations of health took me on a short vacation. He was his own inconsistent self. Now in his most exalted mood, full of cheer, optimistic, almost jovial. Now in the depths of despair, ready for death, bitter, reproachful, self-pitying.

These discussions on his sanity were terribly humiliating, but only at intervals did he recognize the humiliation. To go into such an adventure in high spirits, with all the illusions of chivalry, and after an achievement that he regarded as an act of sacrifice, to have the state of his mind questioned was a ridiculous finish to his sublimity.

There are people who invent all manner of stories as to why I gradually drifted apart from Harry. There is no ignoble cause that they have not adduced. That we quarreled over money, that he was jealous, that I neglected him, that there was some mysterious source of disagreement that the trial had not revealed. Speculators in truth have put all these forward, but the rift showed during the days of the lunacy hearings. We were not estranged then. Indeed, we had many happy days

146

together, even after he was committed to the asylum, but I saw the beginning of the end, and what is more, I recognized that it was indeed the end of my love for Harry Thaw.

In those days of anxiety I had many friends—rumor credits me with more than I possessed—but rumor is a willing creditor. They were friends who grew in a night from mere acquaintanceship. My mailbag was packed every morning with letters and cablegrams from people whom I had never known. My affairs were everybody's affairs, and the temptation to offer advice that carried no responsibilities to the adviser was irresistible. There were letters from people who wanted to help me, letters from good folk who prayed for me—letters from men and women who desired my autograph—my photograph, my clothes, and letters from folk who desired only to give.

I know it is the pose of people who find themselves placed as I was placed that such letters are a nuisance. To me many of these letters, written by warm-hearted and unknown friends, were a source of encouragement and strength. My own countrymen and countrywomen were with me in that tragic period of my life, and I would be the veriest *poseur* to pretend that this knowledge was not immensely helpful. It would serve no useful purpose to reproduce the letters here, but I give one in order to indicate the direction in which public feeling went—

DEAR MADAM.—
I have not the pleasure of knowing you, but feel that I must sit down and write you. Have followed the course of these long trials closely, and realize the extent of your courage and devotion to Harry K. Thaw. Without going into the merits of the case, I appreciate, and I am sure all my fellow citizens appreciate, the terrible ordeal through which you are passing, and I feel it a duty, as one holding public office, to express to you on behalf of my friends and myself a sense of our admiration.
Faithfully,
"— , Mayor,"

This is a representative letter. They came from every grade of society, and were in striking contrast to outpourings of the vicious and decadent men against whose calumny I have had to contend.

The distinction between fame and notoriety is to be found in the character of the stories that are invented concerning the subject. Those of my friends who thought well of me place me among the immortals to my embarrassment, and such inventions as were made, such anecdotes as were created, were eminently flattering. To a jaundiced section, which drew unkindly conclusions, I was less than pleasant, and the stories that found currency were rather awful. But they came when I was in a condition of mind to meet them, and they have made little or no impression.

Like some one else, experts had insulted me, and the amateur efforts of lesser people left me unmoved. I had heard of a man holding quite an important position in his profession openly boasting of his conquest before a dinner party of men, but a man who would take that course of advertising his powers of fascination would lie anyway. There were bitter attacks upon me from many quarters, but that was to be expected. Harry's act and the trial that followed revealed some of the dark spots in the life of New York's fashionable men. White was not alone in his perversity. He was merely the central pivot of a vicious circle. The murder that shocked America, shocked to a greater extent a few Americans, and some found it convenient to leave the country on a visit to Europe. Some stayed on and spent every effort to discredit me, because by discrediting me they might weaken any evidence I might offer against them. I had no intention of moving against them, or of dragging their names into the case, but they did not know this, and they were the people who invented and circulated all that ingenuity could devise to my discredit. For years afterward I found myself coming across these stories. I found that they were believed, and that no explanation or denial on my part could shake the credulity of the people who believed in them. People would say in their kindest manner,

"Oh, yes—but that is all past now—don't let us talk about it."

I know of no more exasperating experience than to be forgiven for an offence that one has not committed. There were other people who had less cause to do me injury, and from their own senseless desire for notoriety, or in a spirit of "fun" caused me a great deal of annoyance—more annoyance, indeed, than any of the inventors of diabolical "incidents" have ever caused me.

Here is a case in point. A girl went down to Salt Lake City; Hired a suite at the best hotel, and with her friends painted the city of the saints the brightest vermilion for a week. She inscribed her name on the register as Evelyn Thaw. Her behavior caused some stir—which is putting the matter very mildly. But one day at the height of the excitement a journalist who had sat through the trials saw her.

To be exact, a local reporter pointed her out.

"That is Evelyn Thaw," he said, and my friend raised his eyebrows. "She is no more Evelyn Thaw than I am," he said, and then and there the impersonation collapsed. The girl admitted that she had taken the name in frolic. Sometimes I found these incidents amusing. The case quoted was not a solitary example by any means. I needed some diversion (though I could have chosen other forms of amusement had the choice been mine), for Harry's case did not end with his incarceration in Mattawan. Indeed, the Thaw case can never end to everybody's satisfaction. I was a constant visitor to the asylum. Harry was treated with every consideration. He had a room of his own, had all the books and comforts which he required, and was given every facility for seeing me alone, both in the asylum and outside. He was allowed to take long motor trips with his warders, and I have been with him quite alone for hours at a stretch.

# CHAPTER XIV
## ON LOVE

I still loved him—I was sorry for him, and pity retains love even as it creates it. There were moments when the old love and comradeship which had been ours in the happiest days of our associations rekindled, and I have recollections of happy as well as most unhappy moments amidst the grim and repressive surroundings of Mattawan. Did you still love a madman? You ask. Did you retain affection for a man so inconsistent, so self-absorbed; so great an egotist as was Harry Thaw? I answer yes. Love does not die all of a sudden. It fades in patches—there were still patches that appealed to me very strongly. No woman possessing womanly feelings can be a eugenist[12] in practice, however much she may be convinced of the sanity of eugenic principles in theory. Reason would depopulate the world, but no human brain can uplift itself to comprehend the greater Reason of Nature. The puny logic of humanity can run with Nature's scheme just so far and no farther—sooner or later it finds itself in conflict with the dominant logic and goes ignominiously to the wall.

There are no apologies for the continuance of relationships other than purely business relationships with Harry. To cut him off because he was a life prisoner of the State—as to all intents and purposes he was—would have been wicked. To change my attitude even in the slightest degree would have been cruel.

Though he tried my patience, though he was at times brutal, though there were moments when the patch of love glowed very feebly, I was a good and faithful wife to him. But I could not continue giving, giving, giving. The everlasting strain was sapping me—destroying me. There were times when I could have screamed from sheer nerves at the futility of his talk; of the extraordinary absence of any sense of proportion he played.

---

[12] Relating or adapted to the production of good or improved offspring.

My own position was a desperate one. Financially I was insecure. The money that came to me came in small sums and at irregular intervals. There are people who imagine that I was in receipt of a princely income, but I think the following letter will give some idea of the efforts that were necessary to secure anything like an adequate allowance from Harry and his people. Sometimes the money did not come to me direct but through a third party, as instance the following, which was sent to a doctor —

Mrs. Evelyn Thaw, New York, N.Y.

June 22$^{nd}$. 1909.

MY DEAR MRS. THAW,—

I received you letter. Will you not be kind enough to send me that tailor's bill again? I am ashamed to ask you the second time, but it was mislead.

        Yours respectfully,

        C. Morshauser.


Dr. Valdemar Sillo, 353 West 57$^{th}$ Street,

New York City, N.Y.

June 26$^{th}$, 1909.

MY DEAR DOCTOR,—

I herewith enclose check for 200 dollars and also 70 dollars for Mrs. Evelyn Thaw. I am arranging to get the 500 dollars, so she can go on a trip, but do not feel that she ought have this unless she shows some symptom of treating Mr. Thaw fair. Do you think if I should send the money she would go on a little trip, and do you think she would see Dr. Meyer?

        Very truly yours,

(Signed) C. Morshauser."

Dr. Meyer was one of Thaw's alienists who evidently wanted to see me very much. Previously he had made several efforts to do so through Mr. O'Reilly. Next, Dr. Sillo called me on the telephone and asked me if I would like to go on a vacation, to which I replied in the affirmative. He then asked if I would be willing to see Dr. Meyer; this I naturally refused. A few days later Dr. Sillo again called me on the telephone, this time saying he had the 500 dollars from Morshauser and would send it to me on condition I would agree to write him a note thanking him for "the arrangements he had made for my vacation" and not to mention the money.

Accordingly I wrote him the following note—

Dr. Valdemar Sillo, 353, West 57th Street,
New York City.

Sunday, July 11th, 1909.
Dear DR. SILLO,—

I want to thank you for the arrangements you have made for my vacation. I start tonight and will let you know how I am getting on. You know how much I need a change of scene. Hope you have a pleasant summer.

"Very sincerely,
"Evelyn Thaw."

I reproduce these only because they give a better idea of the grudging character of the allowances that were made to me. They were written at a time when relationships between the Thaws and myself were very strained, but they are expressive of the attitude that was adopted toward me by the family when money came up for consideration. There were in the course of the years intervening between the murder of Stanford White and the birth of my baby: two trials and four habeas corpus proceedings, so that it may be said that I was occupied for the greater part of three years in strenuous litigation. Such intervals as were left me I devoted to that side of art that

153

appealed to me — modeling in clay. I had always had a leaning in this direction, and I found in the pursuit of my hobby a relaxation that was as necessary as it was pleasant.

I had few illusions about anybody and fewest about myself. At the conclusion of the second trial, with the knowledge that my name and my life had been dragged through the mire, I sat down to reason out my position. And to assist the reasoning I had collected the records of every great criminal trial that had been heard in the past fifty years. There was invariably "a woman in the case." That goes without saying. It was the woman who interested me — the woman guilty or innocent temptress or victim. She and her future were immensely interesting to me. What happened to her when the trial ended, when all the grim figures of tragedy had gone hence and the encores of the case had ceased to reverberate? I spent time and money to find out. And my discoveries were of a depressing nature, for every woman had gone down, down, down. Drink, drugs, the hundred and one wild diversions which eclipse sorrow and soothe heartache had been pressed to service, and the poor light had flickered out dully and miserably. And this without exception. It was a shocking act, but I faced it. Not only were these women the victims of fortune's caprice, but in the vast majority of cases, the innocent victims. Their innocence did not save them from ignominy.

Said I to myself, "Evelyn Thaw, you shall do better than that."

The way of life is full of sharp twists and turnings, each of which reveal vistas which go to the changing of all previous conceptions, making almost nothing of the experiences of the past and demanding clamorously the exercise of new standards and newer and keener application for the future.

The first of the turnings led me to the studios, the second led me to the stage, the third came sharply after my meeting with Stanford White, the fourth followed the tragedy, and the fifth was the birth of Russell.

154

I have endeavored to avoid, in the course of this life, being in any way sentimental. For sentimentality I have the greatest horror, but I say this — whatever be the tag that is attached to my utterance — that a little child is the greatest and the most wonderful gift that life holds, and because of Russell Thaw I found a larger life confronting me. He brought me to a realization of just where I stood in the world, and he called insistently for my return to work.

Throughout my married life I have studied with one ambition — to return to the stage, but I was not in a position to discuss my thoughts with any person in sympathy with my project.

I had recognized my own limitations, I knew that it was out of the question to return to the stage as a chorus girl; I was equally satisfied in my own mind that I could not go back as a principal unless I developed whatever talent was within me. So I bided my time and waited for the maturity that would come to me and would give me the necessary powers. I have said before that I had no illusions; least of all about myself. I knew what was required of an actress. I knew just how far I could go with the equipment that was mine. I had conscientiously pursued a course of study that has broadened my knowledge and sharpened my perception. With the tragic happening which so drastically changed my life all my plans and thoughts slipped out of my mind, and when, after the weary years of trial, I found myself again reaching a normal condition, I was confronted with the fact, that however genuine were my ambitions, I could not now fulfill them without laying myself open to the charge of utilizing the notoriety for my financial benefit that I obtained during the trial. It was a maddening situation, because the stage particularly appealed to me.

I received offers in shoals to make my appearance, not only on the variety (or the vaudeville) stage, but also in serious drama, but to all these I gave an uncompromising "No" in answer. As a woman desires to be loved for herself alone, so I think every artist desires recognition only for the sake of his art. I* can imagine no more trying experience than to be boomed not for the best part of genius which is within one, but for some extraneous cause over which the subject has no control.

Loyalty to Harry, yes, and loyalty to his family prevented my accepting any of the very tempting offers that were made to me, and I think loyalty to myself played as great apart as any. It was not in accordance with my ideas of the fitness of things that a woman who had played so tragic a part in one of the most famous trials of the century, who had moved in the very atmosphere of tragedy, should exhibit herself to a crowd that has no other interest than the interest which morbid human nature gives to those who have suffered in public. Through all the years that followed the trial in the Courts, the offers from theatrical managers came with monotonous regularity.

But if I returned to the stage I was determined that it should not be to the American stage— at first. There were people who thought that I carried my scruples too far. The world is full of people who take a different view from us. On my return to America with Russell, the offers were renewed. Sometimes they would come in the form of very precise business letters, sometimes my return to the stage would form the subject of an after dinner conversation, but I saw no way out of my difficulty. I was having a rather strenuous time, the stores' supplies had failed, and though an heiress under Harry Thaw's will, I was dependent, to a very large extent, upon my own efforts, both for my own livelihood and for the comfort of my child.

Modeling in clay may bring one prizes, may even produce a small income, but I saw no prospect of making good with my hobby. A woman friend invited me to go to Europe and stay with her in Paris. I very gladly accepted the invitation.

I went aboard the *Olympic* without any thought of a stage engagement, without any ideas to what the future in Europe held for me, just vaguely conscious that before me lay one of the crucial moments of my life.

I had lived on hopes and dreams of properties for six years. I have seen myself with the world at my feet and all the prizes that women dearly cherish almost within my grasp, only to be snatched rudely away from me not through any fault of mine.

I had heard myself lauded and execrated, I had been through the trails, been through the very flames to save the life of the man who has now repudiated me. I was starting a new life under new conditions and with no other help but what my own nimble feet could give me. For I was ever a dancer, and I had what a great American producer called "happy feet."

Standing on the deck of the *Olympic* I watched New York fade in the distance with mingled feelings. This was my last visit to Europe; the first had been with Harry Thaw, the second I had left America quietly, sick and miserable, and this was the third. With a sick heart I speculated upon what lay over the ocean's rim for me.

# CHAPTER XV
# THE NEW LIFE

There was a merry party aboard. The boat was crowded, and there were many people whom I knew. Among others were a number of theatrical managers and agents, who were taking their annual trip to Europe.

Looking over my diary I came upon the page that coincided with my departure. Upon it is written—

THE PHILOSOPHY OF EVELYN THAW,

and I reproduce the scraps of philosophy—original and otherwise—which formed my equipment for the struggle that lay ahead of me:

- In France the men are gallant; in England they are good sportsmen. It means the same, but the gallantry of the Englishman is of a more robust type.

- The most unpopular verse in the Scriptures is "Let he who is without fault cast the first stone"; it limits the range of criticism.

- Nothing cultivates a sense of honor so assuredly as a big trouble.

- Happy is the woman who can say, "I know the worst that can happen to me—I've had it."

- The devil would be blacker than he is painted if a lawyer did the painting.

- Plain women often have plain sailing; pretty women find the sea of life pretty rough.

- If I had my choice whether I would be born beautiful and wicked or plain and good, I should not be born at all.

- If I could live my life over again I would only avoid the follies that had unpleasant consequences.

- Passion is an indication of defective capacity.

- All easy ways are downhill; you don't notice it till you start right in to climb back.

- Women's steps are hell ward, because men are the road makers.

- A pretty woman who wants work is offered love; a plain woman who wants love gets the darning.

- People always look for a woman in a scandal — there's no need to look for the man, he's in the spotlight all the time.

- Women can live without loving, but not without being loved.

- I think a child is the most terrible happiness life offers.

- Great publics have an infinite capacity for taking the wrong view.

- Modesty has a jumping off place with every woman.

- Some folks spell "love" with a capital L, and some with a small letter; it is a question of age. I have reached the period of life where I draw a line underneath—just as you do with any other foreign word.

- It is harder to please the low brow than the high brow. It is always the man who has just jumped on his wife who hisses at stage villainy the loudest.

- It is much easier to be rich than strong, and much better to be strong than rich. Moderation is a word that has no significance to the idle rich; they play the "no limit" game, and that's a game in which somebody is surely skinned.

- The way out of life is trouble; the way out of trouble is work.

- It isn't fair to sneer at the virtuous—everybody isn't interesting.

- Temptation is a two-handed game—it requires one player and a dummy.

- Popularity isn't a matter of justice—it's a matter of sympathy. Many a good man or woman deserves popularity who have only got respect.

- It is a terrible thing to be respected—it implies a multitude of "buts."

- A fellow feeling is a term that implies recognition of one's own weakness in others. We never have fellow feeling about virtues.

- The entire world loves a lover, save one of the lover's parents.

- The worst thing a woman can do is to do nothing. Nature abhors a vacuum and the world does not love passive sinners.

- In a man "love" is a word that comes as easily as "damn" later.

- When a woman is faithful to man people say, "It pays her to be."

- The woman who imputes the worst motive to men is so seldom wrong that she is apt to get a swollen head.

- Some women are like frosted stone; they repel even the opposite sex by their coldness and harness. I never see such women with children without marveling how it happened. Other women are like flames—they burn themselves up between lunch and breakfast time.

- Beware of the disinterested man who wants to help you; pay cash—it will come cheaper in the long run.

- Regrets are useless. You can't repair the foundations from the roof.

- The monk who looked for the Philosopher's Stone and found gunpowder was conducting an experiment that all women of all ages have been essaying.

- I never regret my life. It would mean regretting much happiness.

- You may do anything in this world so long as you do not reduce your actions to words. Printers' ink is the seal of damnation.

- When a man says a woman is deficient he means that she cannot get down to his level.

- There are certain subjects that one possessing any sense of delicacy cannot touch upon. Except in the sketchiest manner.

I have found myself getting further and further away from the Thaws. I have never been in sympathy with them, and Harry was the only link that bound me to a quite impossible situation.

Harry was a man who was easily influenced in some things. His self-appreciation went a long way to securing his confidence, and the faith in his judgment, which was never absent, was intensified and strengthened by sycophancy and the flattery of approval.

It was necessary for his sake and for mine that I should present to him a truthful and a wholesome view of the ever-changing situation as I found it.

There were easy ways for me to find oblivion, but I had determined upon working out my salvation in such a manner so that I could avoid the fate which has awaited other women similarly circumstanced, and had led their way to an ignominious end.

My position was a trying one. I was hard pressed for money. Harry's baby was coming along, and I had to endure, in addition to the other trials that had awaited me, the vilest of suggestions as to the child's paternity.

The breach was widening. Every day my relationship with Harry and his family became more unendurable. The strain was beginning to tell upon me, and with the last shock I began to break down.

The awfulness of the innuendoes and suggestions, more especially in regard to my little unborn child, drove me almost to frenzy. I wanted to get away; I wanted to hide myself and forget the name of Thaw; to forget everything that had gone before; I wanted to leave all the scenes of my humiliation, to bury myself in some place where I should not be known, some sleepy hollow to which the very thoughts could not penetrate.

I was desperately hard up, and but for the supreme kindness of one good friend I do not know how I should have gone through the ordeal.

I have met men in this world, good men and bad men and men who were neither wholly good nor wholly bad, and this last classification is by far the more numerous, so that when one meets either of the extremes one meets a very interesting personality.

It was my good fortune to enjoy the friendship of a man who was wholly good, who was neither depraved, or prudish, a broad-minded friend who recognized how terrible was my position, and who assisted me to leave America for Europe, where in Germany Russell Thaw was born.

What I was to do in the future I could not quite see clearly. I had hopes of continuing my studies of sculpture in Paris, but I knew I could not expect to make as great a living at that.

The position was a very serious one for me, as I have already said. I doubt that any period of my life was so serious. It promised to be an uninteresting voyage in spite of the cheery company aboard, yet that trip on the *Olympic* was one of the most fateful I have ever tasted.

Seated opposite to me at breakfast I noticed one morning a young-looking man. He had a very dark complexion, and I thought at first that he was Italian, and I was very much surprised when later I heard him speaking English. There was nothing about him to suggest that he was, in any way, associated with theatrical business, and indeed my first impression of him was that he was a young Italian gentleman returning from a trip to the States.

I noticed him with the curiosity that an idle passenger may devote to a fellow traveler. One afternoon I asked somebody with whom I had seen him speaking who he was. "That is Albert de Dourville," replied my friend. "He is the manager of the London Hippodrome, and he is very keen on your appearing under his management."

It was a novel idea to me. It never seriously occurred to me that I should return to the stage in London. And yet it opened a vista that was particularly agreeable to me. In England, I was an unknown quantity, the echoes of the trial and had died down. They had forgotten possibly that I had ever lived, and certainly my appearance there would not rouse the prejudice, and the very natural prejudice, which is devoted to the notoriety hunter. Later in the day, I was introduced to Mr. De Courville, and after that time we discussed every matter under the sun except my return to the stage. "How would you like to appear at the Hippodrome?"

The Hippodrome was only a name to me, but I gathered that it was something like the Hippodrome in New York.

"I think I should like it," I said hesitatingly.

I did not know even then what I wanted to do. There was still within me that shrinking from publicity, and reluctance to make capital out of my tremble that had prevented me from appearing in New York.

"It is worth while considering," said Mr. De Courville, and I agreed. No more was said about it. I saw him once or twice that evening and the next morning, but for the moment I was engaged with yet another little shock that had come to me. Harry Thaw had publicly repudiated his own son Russell, and a wireless to that effect had reached the ship.

I think that distressed me more than anything that had happened in the previous years — since that terrible day when Jerome put me on the stand.

Mr. De Courville was most sympathetic. I had tentatively agreed with Mr. Marinelli, the agent, to appear under De Courville's management at a large salary. It was after the arrival of that Marconigram that Mr. De Courville very generously increased the salary, although, through Marinelli, we had mutually agreed upon the sum.

My reply then to Harry Thaw, and to all who cast the slightest doubt upon the paternity of Russell, is that no man who has seen Harry Thaw and seen Russell can have the slightest doubt as to the child's parentage. I signed the contract to appear at the Hippodrome and reached England with a comfortable sense that at last I was going into strenuous work in a country where my name was practically unknown, and where no one would care whether I appeared or not.

My faith in my obscurity was to be rudely shaken, for no sooner had I reached England, and the announcement of my engagement had been made public, than the newspapers began to get busy.

I did not accompany my friends to London but went straight on to Paris. I was blissfully unconscious that my arrival had created any stir in Europe, but on the day the *Olympic* reached England an announcement had been made in one of the evening papers in London that I had been engaged at a salary of a little more than I was actually getting. As I say, I knew nothing of this, and went on to Paris, where I found a quiet hotel and registered as Evelyn Nesbit.

I did this because, however pathetic the European journalist might be as to my presence and my plans, I had no doubt whatever that my expressed intention of returning to the stage would excite some comment in America, and the American reporter is ubiquitous.

On Monday morning following my arrival, my agent called me up on the telephone from London.

"There is going to be some opposition to your appearing at the Hippodrome," he said.

"Why?" I asked.

"Because," he explained, "there is a suggestion that your engagement is due rather to the desire of management of the Hippodrome for notoriety than to any desire on their part to secure a competent artiste."

"Who is making the trouble?" I asked.

"The *Daily Sketch*," was the reply.

The next day the paper arrived, and I thought that the comments upon my reappearance were, to say the least, very unkind. The whole case was recalled, and there was a cartoon that did not err, in my opinion, on the side of charity. Nevertheless, the letterpress was fair from the point of view of the editor, and I for one agreed that it was very undesirable that any person should be on the stage for no other reason than because he or she had earned some dubious kind of fame in a *cause célèbre*.

There was, too, some justification for the editor's suspicion that I was making my appearance on the strength of the part I had played before the trial. After all, I had not been on the stage as a principal; I had never appeared in the role that I had now engaged myself to play. I had never done solo dances, though my passion for dancing was well known in New York.

But if the position was serious for me, it was much more serious for the Hippodrome management and Mr. De

Courville. The Hippodrome had a reputation for quietness and had an audience that was remarkable to its tone.

As I have said before, the attitude of the paper was perfectly logical. It said in effect: "If Mrs. Thaw is to appear on the stage for no other reason than because she is the wife of a man who is, at the present moment, a convicted murderer, where will this form of engagement end?" (I might say in parentheses, that Harry Thaw is not a convicted murderer for he has been found "Not Guilty" of the charge of murdering Stanford White. I mention this in passing: I intended to refer to it at an earlier stage in the book.)

As I began to realize that I also reflected some of the apprehension felt in London. It was a rude awakening to my dream. I had become optimistic and my heart was in the task that I had set myself, and here it seemed that I was to be baulked at the very threshold of my new career.

It is the pose of a certain class, and by a certain type of intelligence, to sneer at the influence that is exercised by the Press.

But, for my own part, I have a respect that amounts almost to awe for the extraordinary nature of that power.

The *Daily Sketch* view was a sane view, as I have said. It was difficult, however, to explain to the editor all the circumstances that had led up to my arrival in Paris and my engagement at the Hippodrome. For all the people in London knew or cared, I had come straight from the trial to make an appearance on a variety stage. They were not interested in all that had happened since the trial; the intervening space between the last of the tribunal trials and my arrival in Europe was a blank to them. I might be drawing a fabulous income from the Thaws for all they knew. My position was a delicate one. I had made it a rule never to engage in any form of controversy with a newspaper. I had recognized that of all futile forms of amusement, that of running your head against the products of modern journalism is the most futile.

There was nothing to do but to sit and wait. I was misunderstood, and it was difficult to explain. Mr. De Courville had been in communication with the editor of the *Daily Sketch*, but I do not think that the paper was convinced as to the necessity for my appearing. De Courville and I discussed the matter over the telephone, "I'm determined that you shall appear, and I am equally anxious that you shall appear without any misapprehension existing on the part of the *Daily Sketch* or any other newspaper as to why you are coming," said Mr. De Courville. "The paper is not satisfied as to the genuineness of this engagement or the necessity for it. I have asked them to send a representative to see you, to judge for himself."

It was on a Sunday morning that the *Daily Sketch* man arrived — he came long before I was awake, for he had traveled all night to see me. It was not a novel experience this business of being interviewed, but this was to be a momentous experience, for upon the impression that was formed depended the attitude of the *Daily Sketch* and incidentally my return to the stage.

It was a pleasant interview. The obvious sincerity of the journal to preserve its public from anything approaching sensationalism stripped me of resentment.

I was frank, for I find that frankness is the one quality which pays in dealing with the British journalist, and my interviewer returned to London with the story that made my appearance possible.

Shall I ever forget those weeks of preparation for my return to the stage? They were partly spent in Paris, where Mr. De Courville had secured for me the assistance of Jack Clifford, a famous dancer, whose experience had ranged from San Francisco to Paris.

This was a very wise provision. Jack Clifford had been chosen because of his extraordinary muscularity and because

Mr. De Courville thought that if stage fright got the better of me, Clifford would be able to carry me through my act.

Dresses were ordered specially for the number in which I was to appear. A dancing master was brought from Italy to arrange my entrance, and the chorus of "*Hullo! Ragtime!*" was specially rehearsed to make it as effective as possible. Indeed, all that could possibly be done to make my entrance effective was done. Nevertheless every day that passed made me more and more nervous.

When it seemed that my return might be the signal for demonstrations by people who knew little of the circumstances, and who might resent my return, the management determined upon a course that was at once novel and ingenious. They cabled to America to send twenty American girls of my color and size. If the opposition had be as great as he feared I was to make my appearance with these girls, and the audience must guess as to which of the twenty-one was Evelyn Thaw.

My arrival in the theatre coincided with the arrival of the girls, but the opposition had died down and there only remained the fear that I should not make good upon my appearance. This was fear that I shared.

The fatal day arrived. It was a Saturday afternoon. No previous announcement had been made that I was to return upon that day. All the advertising had been to the effect that I should come into the cast on the following Monday.

The curtain went up. The play proceeded, and went so smoothly that the applause and laughter came ringing back to where I stood, a forlorn figure I fear, at the back of the stage.

I was not due to make my appearance until the last act, and quickly as the revue ran it seemed to drag out to an interminable length.

Friends came and spoke encouragingly to me. Everybody was most charming, but nevertheless I could not share his or her optimism.

169

I seized an opportunity that presented itself, and went away behind some scenery and sat down.

In that ten minutes I viewed my life, and the tragic turbulence of it, my first introduction to the stage, my meeting with White, the sorrow and misery that followed; Harry Thaw in his Matteawan cell rose before my eyes, the tragic comedy of his quixotic impulses and consummation had his obsession; the trial, the keen-faced, remorseless Jerome, the home in Pittsburgh with all its atmosphere of narrowness, and here was I at the end of all endeavor, at the end of all fond hopes and dreadful fears, with my foot again upon the threshold of a career.

I rose with a sense of determination, with a sense of triumph, and I had stepped out on to the stage as the callboy came running up to me. "Your number, Miss Nesbit," he said, and as the orchestra crashed the opening bars of "I'm simply crazy about some boy!" I stepped out to the glare of the footlights, realizing just who that boy was and how much his future depended upon my success.

## THE END